OL

D0915923

IP 83
10 ⁰⁰
00

Apprenticeship on the Couch

Years of
Apprenticeship
on the Couch

Tilmann Moser
Fragments of my Psychoanalysis

INTRODUCTION BY HEINZ KOHUT

Translated from the German by Anselm Hollo

Urizen Books   *New York*

Copyright © Suhrkamp Verlag Frankfurt am Main 1974
Translation © Urizen Books New York 1977

No part of this publication may be reproduced, stored in a retrieval system, or transmitted, in any form or by any means, electronic, mechanical,
photo-copying, recording or otherwise, without prior written permission
of the publisher.

Printed in the United States of America
Composition by Morning Star Press

Library of Congress Cataloging in Publication Data

Moser, Tilmann, 1938-
  Years of apprenticeship on the couch.

  Translation of Lehrjahre auf der Couch.
  1. Psychoanalysis—Biography.   2. Moser,
Tilmann, 1938-   I. Title
RC506.M6913 616.8'917'0924 [B] 76-58387

ISBN 0-916354-45-8

Content

Dedicated to my patient analyst

Introduction

Dear Friend Moser:

So you want me to write an introduction to your book. Well, I can't deny it: I did, some time ago, declare myself willing to provide one. After first reading your manuscript in the fall of 1972, I was sufficiently impressed by it to volunteer an introduction. Now, however, after all this time, I do not find myself quite so ready, and approach the task with greater hesitation. I am, in fact, half tempted to beg off with a joke, telling you that if *The Apprenticeship of Wilhelm Meister* could make it into print without an introduction, surely Tilmann Moser's *Apprenticeship* can do likewise. But I do not want to shirk the task. My perspective has probably improved with the passing of months since that first reading, the initial enthusiasm having given way to a cooler, if still well-tempered, benevolence towards your record. Now I see many things more clearly which militate against your work, or at least seem to be doing so. As others may be affected by similar doubts, I think I can help your cause best by examining, and responding to, those misgivings. I am convinced that your book deserves such assistance.

Well, then, what objections can be raised against your confessions? Let me begin in my capacity of analyst, an old and experienced analyst. This may be of some importance to you, as you are a young analyst, and undoubtedly feel insecure when told by older colleagues that your undertaking, the description of your analysis—your own training analysis, at that—is, analytically speaking, suspect, especially considering that you devoted yourself to this literary endeavor *during* your analysis as well as after its conclusion.

3

I have thought a great deal about the conclusion of analyses and have written a number of things on the subject. And if you had asked me, say, ten years ago, for my opinion of an analysis that concludes with the analysand's recording the history of his analysis, and his intention of publishing it, I certainly would not have hesitated very long before voicing my opinion that something must have gone wrong in that analysis. A good analysis, I would have told you, ends in a state of sorrow—the analysand's sorrow over the final and irrevocable relinquishing of the childhood ties that have been re-experienced in their transference to the analyst. After the conclusion of an analysis, after the conclusion of a good analysis, I would have said that the analysand is so engrossed in coming to terms with his separation from the analyst and with his separation from the great figures of his childhood that he cannot muster much surplus energy for other tasks. True, the *inner* work on the analysis certainly ought to continue for a while after its conclusion—but a report on what has taken place, and particularly, a report addressed to the general public, is surely a form of acting out, of repeating infantile experience through action, and *not*, as should be the case in a good analysis, a remembering and a coming to terms with the realization that those conflicts and reactions have no place in adult life.

Today, I think differently, and you know it, and probably have made that knowledge your own in both theoretical and practical terms. As long as it is a matter of infantile attachments, of infantile loving and hating, it is quite correct to assume that an acting out of these attachments instead of an understanding of them—understanding that they no longer have a place in adulthood—certainly indicates that not everything has been brought to its proper conclusion in the analysis. I do not want to go into technical detail: even here, there are exceptions, but generally speaking, this assumption is the right one.

It does not, however, hold true, not even in principle, when the analytical effort has been directed primarily to the problems of a disturbance of self-esteem. One might regard the relinquishing of old concepts of one's own greatness as analogous to the relinquishing of parental and sibling attachments in an analysis of the other main category. And it is true that the analysand experiences a kind of sorrow over the loss of the old idealized image of strength and perfection with which he had once wanted to merge. Yet something else happens in these

4

analyses that is unparalleled in the others: a gradual transformation of the greatness that we once felt we possessed—directly or by partaking in the power that we ascribed to the great figures to which we looked up in our childhood—a gradual increase of creative initiative, an increment of creative urge and liberated creative powers in talents that existed only sketchily prior to the analysis (this mostly being the case ever since the analysand's adolescence) and which are now fueled by the tremendous, newly transformed powers of erstwhile infantile self-regard. I am tempted to expound some more on these possibilities, but feel compelled to stop. I am not writing a book, but just an introduction to one.

The second objection that occurs to me concerns the question whether the description of an analysis to the public—*your* description of *your* analysis to the public—does not violate the subtle laws of good taste. I must confess that I find this question of greater import than the technical one concerning the correct conclusion of analytical work. Some boundaries are hard to define. The problems of differentiation between what is ugly and obscene, and what is indicative of openly joyful sexual freedom, are closely related to that with which I am here concerned. Decisions in this area depend on many different kinds of factors, and are, in all likelihood, bound to be relativistic. The writer's intention—whether he wants to cause a 'sensation', or whether his confessions are based on other, more sublime motivations—is certainly very important, but it is not everything. It is possible to write with good intentions and nevertheless call forth experiences in the reader that belong to a much lower emotional realm than the one the author knew himself to be at home in. In a certain respect, the emotional situation created in analysis does resemble its counterpart in sexual love. In both cases, we develop an intense feeling toward another person; in both situations the presence of a third person destroys the essence of the experience. The presence of a third or of an even greater number of others leads either to a flattening-out of the emotions, or to their primitivization. A love relationship becomes a sexual orgy. The analytical twosome turns into a tense social group where the inflamed instincts of the participants will not be pacified by verbal expression but clamor for action.

Essentially, the psychoanalytical situation is a private one. It represents a human being's attempt to be honest with himself, to understand with increasing clarity what it is that he had formerly repudiated in himself. He learns to look at the unaccepted part of himself as a first step on the road to changing it. His own feeling of shame is often so great that he can persist in this labor only with the benevolent assistance of another person. The idea that there are many benevolent others who could give assistance, a benevolent public which could help one bear the shame, does not, to my mind (and rightly so), belong to the general realm of modern man's expectations.

However, my dear friend Moser, I feel quite certain that the publication of your report on your analysis does not in any way violate the limits of good taste. I do believe that many will turn to your book with the expectation of satisfying their unsublimated curiosity, that some will buy it with the (admitted or unadmitted) intention to find the reading sexually stimulating. But I do not believe that your book will be found satisfactory in these respects. Here, all does depend on the author's manner of procedure. Form is what divides art from obscenity. Whatever your motivations were that drove you to reveal your experiences to the reading public, it was not crude exhibitionism. You have experienced something in your analysis, something great, self-expanding, that you want to share with others, many others, with the world. The book's message—and in places, it still is too personified to my taste—concerns the healing power of analysis, the healing, beneficial power of self-scrutiny, the positive, liberating, ultimately and actively creative salutariness of that process. We only have to add something to this—and I am sure it is something that was instrumental in creating your wish to undertake the writing of this book—namely, that it has to be the *right kind* of analysis, based on an understanding of your individuality, and not some psychological Bed of Procrustes on which the analysand has to submit to the formal concepts and rules of some preconceived notions.

If that is the message, if I have read you right, then this also explains why the question of 'good taste' becomes irrelevant. Your book is an enthusiastic book, a testimony. Perhaps—and this may be an example of the ironies inherent in the workings of the unconscious processes—you have, at the end of your rejection of your de-idealized father, returned to the fathers once again; arrived, from the rejected sermon of the grand-paternal spiritual pastor, at the sermonizing description of the saving of souls in another realm. Perhaps you wanted to give the many a message of healing, after you yourself had successfully gotten rid of that message of salvation.

I do not want to pursue these uncertain and perhaps too playful interpretations too far. Whatever the foundations of your enthusiasm—enthusiasm for your analyst, for the analytical researchers, beginning with Freud, who have contributed to the progress of the analytical science, and for the entire structure of psychoanalysis, and for the analytical process itself—I feel a sense of clear and strong gratitude for your very ability to be enthusiastic. I do regret, deeply, that an entire younger generation, succeeding mine—that the best of this young generation seem to have lost that ability. This may well be a reaction against the gullibility of the fathers who let themselves be seduced by the *Führer*. However understandable the excessive urge to objectivity in this generation, it is my belief that it is misdirected. There is nothing wrong with enthusiasm *per se*. Only enthusiasm for wrongdoing is wrong. Without the ability to be enthusiastic, one is soon lost in the world of action. One has to be able to react in the depths of one's soul if one wants to preserve one's integrity within society's grinding gears, and if one wants to be a staunch fighter in support of what is good.

But these reflections lead too far afield. I have to leave them now and turn to the third possible objection, in order to approach the end of this already too-long introduction.

Like the first one, the third objection is of a technical nature. Unlike the first, it does not concern your position as an analysand—it concerns your position as an analyst. Your analysis was not merely a therapeutic one, a healing treatment of your personal ailments, but it was also a learning experience, i.e., a step on your way to becoming a full-fledged analyst. I do of course know that it is possible to claim—and, in a certain sense, quite justifiably—that such a difference does not exist, that each training analysis is nothing but a therapeutic one. That is certainly correct. But from another point of view, this attitude towards the problem of the training analysis is not comprehensive enough. The analysand's intention to become an analyst undoubtedly plays an important part in the psychic transpositions that take place during the analysis and influences, in particular, the way the end of the course of analysis is experienced. The analysand who does not become a psychoanalyst does not have to do anything with his newly gained insights but to use them for his own further life, for the maintenance of his own psychic equilibrium. The psychological discoveries that he has made in himself during the analysis will subsequently be applied only to himself. Not so with the future analyst. After concluding his analysis, he has to take yet another step, sometimes even two. Essentially, his psychic insights have to be detached from himself and directed towards the general,* without, however, shortchanging the personal, the self-personal, in the process. In other words, the insights that the analyst has gained while working on himself have to enable the doctrines of analysis to be experienced not as dry and far removed from life, but as abstractions that can be deduced from experience, or that at least relate to possible experience. The further, third, step would then be the one from the analyst's therapeutic experience in the technical situation with his analysands on to research, i.e., the step from the specific to the general. Here, I want to discuss only one single aspect of those further steps, namely, the question whether the publication of your report on your own analysis might not turn out to be an obstacle in the course of your future therapeutic work.

It is a question to be taken seriously and deserves a serious answer. First, I would like to divide it up into two subordinate questions: 1.) Won't the loss of your anonymity, which will be a result of the publication of the autobiographical account of your analysis, make the analysis of your future analysands more difficult? 2.) Won't the impression your book makes on still hesitating potential patients lead to a situation in which a certain group among them will feel attracted by your personality and thus hasten to consult you, while others will feel repelled by your particular nature and therefore give your office a wide berth?

As far as I can see, the first-mentioned danger is of no great importance. I believe that the narrow interpretation of the theoretically correct maxim that the analyst has to be anonymous and is not allowed to be anything but a mirror, reflecting the impressions that emanate from the patient back to him, is based on a gross, un-psychological error. Theoretically the principle is correct, but neutrality and anonymity do not mean that the analyst is to be devoid of reactions, or that the patient is not permitted to know anything about him. Every analysis automatically establishes a baseline, a stable background, against which the outlines of the analysand's personality and of the fig-

---

* It need hardly be stressed that this maxim also applies to other professions which, like the psychoanalytical, deal with the psychic life of fellow human beings.

ures of his childhood delineate themselves. If, in the analysis, the analyst pays complete attention to the patient, keeps the patient's personality in mind, and, if possible, does not introduce into the analytic situation anything from his own personality but his reactions to the analysand's revelations, then the analytical work proceeds quite unimpeded—regardless of whether the analyst is totally unknown to the analysand, or whether the analysand is familiar with many details of his past and his personality. Every analyst soon learns to recognize the deviations from reality that appear in the analysand's communications, whether it is a question of distortions in perception of the analyst's appearance or personality, or of maladjusted, i.e., exaggerated or of inappropriate reactions towards the interpretations he advances. And every analyst learns not to deny the analysand's correct perceptions nor to disregard the distortions that emanate from the transference. Thus, I do not believe that your analytical confession will harm your patients. On the contrary, I think that your courage, your ability to look down into the psychic depths despite fear, will encourage your analysands as well, not to be ashamed, not to deny anything, thus following the example of psychic courage you yourself have given.

But the second part of the third question seems to me the one of the gravest import, of those that I am trying to respond to here, especially to a young analyst like yourself. I do believe that the publication of your book will lead to a certain selection of your patients, that a certain personality type will feel attracted to yours, and that others will not come to you who otherwise might have done so, even if only after overcoming some hesitation after having made your superficial acquaintance. That is a pity—a pity because a young analyst, initially still caught up in his own problems and tending to see the psychological world too narrowly as patterned like his own, must gradually become acquainted with the full range of man's psychological experiences—many of them quite different from those with which he became acquainted in his own analysis. True, there is no analyst in the world who would feel equally at home among *all* personality types. We all have our limitations (probably limitations that were often determined by experiences in early childhood) beyond which we cannot step without encountering excessive difficulties. Every analyst learns how to avoid certain groups of analysands, either because they depress him too much, make him anxious, or because he is truly unable to understand them. Nevertheless, it is a great pity to see a young analyst be in some way compelled to restrict his experiences in too great a measure at the very beginning of his career. Therein lies a risk, dear Moser, that you have to decide on for yourself. I do of course assume that you have considered it and that you believe that the restriction will not prove all too great. I hope you are right, for your own sake. There is one thing I can tell you here by way of consolation and reassurance. If you do good analytical work, word gets around, and if you understand your patients well, word-of-mouth recommendation will cause even such patients to appear on your doorstep who were perhaps subtly repelled by your book when they read it, or who generally tend to avoid any analyst who is the author of books for the general reading public.

Now I really have to come to a conclusion. It seems best, after all these careful considerations, to break through my own reservations once again and to tell you that your book has made me very happy. As you well know, I am, despite my age, a most enthusiastic psychoanalyst. I believe that analysis is a science with a great future, that it is a science still only taking its first steps. In the time of its origination, the greatest danger it ran was a lack of scientific discipline: and Freud warned at that time against "wild analysis". And although psychoanalysis will soon celebrate its first centennial, that danger is still quite real. Yet I believe that premature senility, a senility of childhood, if I may say so, represents the greater danger today. What psychoanalysis needs today, if it wants to realize its full inherent potential, is courageous analysts, young creative spirits who have understood its essentials without getting stuck in the formal-traditional. That is why your book has given me such pleasure. I found in it something youthfully creative that is entirely compatible with the essentials of the analytical tradition. Thus, at the end of these introductory words, I cannot wish you anything better than that the readers of your book— the enlightened public, future patients, other analysts—will be able to step beyond their preoccupation with this or that detail that they might wish to question; that they will accept it, as I came to do, as evidence of the vitality, the contemporary vitality, of our great and growing science.

Yours,
Heinz Kohut

Foreword

As the final decision whether or not to publish this report drew close, I often woke up at night to nightmarish thoughts about possible consequences of the publication, for myself and others. Therefore, I asked some friends and experienced analytical colleagues for advice: almost all of them voted for publication under a pseudonym. But this I would have found hard to take, not only because of my pride as an author and the then necessary revisions, but also because of the specific nature of my relationship to the described analysis and to the report on it: the book is an affirmation of psychoanalysis, of the analyst, of my neuroses, of *his* way of treating or curing them. What use would such an affirmation be if presented anonymously? Just a game of hide-and-seek. As I had anticipated when I started writing, certain colleagues wagged their heads as soon as they had heard about the manuscript. There were questions as to the legitimacy of the analysis: why hadn't the analyst made a more thorough study of my exhibitionist tendencies? Why hadn't a couple of years passed between the analysis and the writing of the report? etc. A solicitous female colleague passed on the word that my entry in the professional association might be jeopardized.

The manuscript's first reader, a non-analyst, voiced his mortified opinion: "Well, it appears things are just as bad in psychoanalysis as I've always imagined them to be." Thus, the book would discourage him from ever turning to a psychotherapist when overtaken by some psychic disturbance. Will this be the case with many readers? Is the knowledge of how psychoanalysis has worked in a specific case a deterrent from it? This was one of the arguments I had to consider: the prejudices against psychoanalysis might be aggravated among a greater number of people, the resistance become more rigid, the head-shaking and incomprehension grow more massive. Accordingly, the book would do damage to psychoanalysis—merely because it publicizes what happens to someone who submits to a thorough course of it. Did this mean that a veil of secrecy ought to remain drawn over these events, as it was with the occult mysteries which were not to be desecrated by uninvited spectators? The accusation of obscurantism is, of course, an ancient item in the arsenal of those who polemicize against psychoanalysis—*because,* generally, the events in the treatment are only described in theoretical terms and from the analyst's viewpoint. Thus, the argument that it might be damaging to the cause of psychoanalysis if its real, concrete experience were made public appeared to me an utterly un-analytical or even anti-analytical one. Yet I am willing to admit that nothing can protect this book from misreadings.

Another argument: you have to protect your family. But do I damage them if they find out who I am, and if others do? I was warned against the importunate curiosity that would follow me through my subsequent life, against malicious psycho-analytical re-interpretations of this report, against the danger of my being nailed down for ever on my own psychopathology.

Then, there was a truly weighty consideration: at some time, it said, you will have to decide between the occupation of a writer and that of a psychoanalyst. Freud relentlessly hid his private existence from the patients who entrusted themselves to him. The analyst's anonymity is one of the basic principles of psychoanalysis: his anonymity is the projection screen on which the shadow-plays of transference are observed.

This report, I was told, is an aggressive act against all your patients, present and future; their therapy is made more difficult, if not impossible, if they are able to find out all they want about your own neurosis. In difficult transference situations they will wave your own book at you and say: you aren't any different, or: how do you think you can help me? You have had exactly the same problems. Friends advised me to delete at least the "most delicate" passages because they were bound to encourage imaginative fixations in the patients.

Quite clearly, there was a form of wavering in the many consultations (for which I am grateful): between the supposedly immutable guidelines of abstinence and anonymity; between cautiously liberated speculations whether the report might not have a positive, relaxing, encouraging, anxiety-diminishing effect on many current analyses, on one hand, and the individual fears of the dissolution of limits of intimacy, for which there was no justification except for that certain, established distinction between "the public" and "the private," solidified by inner resistance, on the other. It became increasingly obvious that there are no reliable rules for making the distinction between what can and what cannot be said. How much a person is allowed to find out about another without crossing the line of shame; when anyone starts feeling ashamed, or when he *ought to* do so—no one can say. But among people there is at least as much gratuitous shame as there is gratuitous anxiety. The entire book is, in fact, an attempt to deal with the problem of my own feelings of shame.

Yet a serious problem exists only between the analyst and his patient, and it is this: not to know anything about the analyst is a vexation for the patient—but also an opportunity. The opportunity consists in being able to model the analyst according to one's own needs, at least in one's own imagination. Depending on the demands put by the process of transference, he can thus take on reassuring as well as threatening forms. Throughout transference there is, however, a continuous need for identification, and this, with an idealized image of the analyst in which the hurtful restrictions of the parental images are lifted once again, at least in the imagination: during a passing phase, the analyst represents the ideal parents, and this is absolutely necessary for the creation of a stable psychic structure. A young child is unable to comprehend its parents' complete psychic reality, it *has to* distort it, even idealize and glorify it, and where this proves impossible, disturbances result—disturbances that have been increasingly noted in the past years. It appears as if a child were unable to live, at a certain stage, without the belief that the parents are strong, good and not seriously impeded in any way. The later orientation toward the parents' *reality* then becomes a laborious process, propelled by the need to live through disappointments without hatred. Many patients have foundered on their too-early disillusionment with their parents, no matter if this occurred consciously or unconsciously. They have to pass through the phase of a positive or negative idealization of the analyst, according to their deepest needs, so as to let heal the wounds that their disappointment with the parents has caused them. The dissolution of this idealization then takes place during a later stage of the analysis.

The weightiest argument against the publication of this report was, then, that such a massive breach in the analyst's anonymity would disrupt the free unfolding of transference. The unknown analyst's mirror would become a distorting mirror in which the patient would, at first, not see himself, but a more or less concrete image of the analyst with which the patient would then compare himself, finding it repulsive or attractive, but in any case, have to deal with his own reality. The report would interfere with the process of idealization, presenting the patient too soon with the analyst's reality, an "all-too-human" reality, in view of the patient's needs.

Thus, the question is: when, and how, can a patient endure the knowledge of the analyst's psychic and human reality without having his own healing process impeded? There is no general and definitive answer, but I take the opportunity of this foreword to warn my patients not to plunge into this book as soon as they have laid hands on it. Many patients attempt a secret investigation of the analyst's real life, and this is mostly a symptom of violent resistance against the continuation of the analysis. The resistance of my patients can attach itself to this book. Their reading it *may* in certain circumstances deprive me of the chance of really helping them. They will, no doubt, read it at some point in their lives: it is merely a question of postponement and mutual preparation.

Underlying the warnings and reactions of my colleagues is the difficult question whether the analysts, as a rule, succeed in dissolving their idealization toward the end of analysis to a sufficient degree—or whether they do enough, or allow enough to happen, to make that dissolution possible. That dissolution is a difficult process: it is possible to accustom oneself to an only partially deserved admiration, and it may well be that one does not want to accept signs of its diminution with true equanimity. Dependencies of former patients, lasting many years, and permanent fixations on an exaggerated perception of the analyst are not at all rare, nor does this report appear to be entirely lacking in them.

When I discussed these questions with my analyst, a few months after the end of my analysis, he said he sometimes shuddered at the thought of collegial critical comments in view of my record of some of his deviations from orthodox methodical purity in his conduct of the analysis. It was evident that he, too, felt somewhat tempted to plead for pseudonymous publication, on these grounds. But then he decided that he would be able to justify most of it, and to take the criticism: both of us would have to console ourselves—I because I had not been perfectly analyzed, and he, because he had not analyzed me perfectly.

As for the rest, I hope to learn, in time, how to deal with the situation of my patients as changed by this book. Many analysts have been afraid of patients who have read too many books about psychoanalysis before beginning therapy. However, the technical problems their resistances created through book learning can be solved. One must only find the right variables so as to help them despite those barricades, if they really want help; and I hope this book does not cut me off from my potential ability to help.

Some friends and colleagues were struck by the degree to which the report emphasizes the positive transference over the negative; one friend even spoke of an "idolization" of the analyst and urged me to correct it. Whereupon I tried, though unsuccessfully, to re-enter stages of hatred, rage, and scorn which I certainly had experienced. Yet I would like to point out the problem, throughout the analysis, of my devaluation of the analyst: it was a persistent, if not spectacular form of a negative transference, a sneaking aggressivity that did not grant respect to the "opponent" in open conflict, simply declaring him too weak for it. This aggressive diminution of the analyst, though it certainly was less stormy than many phases of affection, ceased only in the last months of analysis.

I would like to add that the sub-title *Fragments of My Psychoanalysis* is intended seriously, though not in the sense of any conscious omissions. I have essentially recorded the *experiences* that had the strongest impact on me, and less of the intellectual knowledge of the genesis and structure of my neurosis. This is no doubt an injustice toward the analysts whose achievement in terms of psychoanalytical enlightenment remains under-represented. It is more a report on the "apprenticeship" of experiencing, less on the training in theoretical comprehension. This comprehension expands in precisely those analytical intervals in which the energy of the psyche does not appear entirely consumed by the force of emotions. Thus I have mainly recorded those interpretations made by the analyst that really "struck home" and moved me over a long period of time.

Finally, a word to the people at the origin of my depression which drove me to psychoanalysis: my parents. It is only too obvious that they in many ways differ greatly from their early shadow images in this book. In professional jargon, this is called the difference between representation and reality. I hope that the book is free from accusations and petulant discontent such as have been my companions for almost three decades, to my own humiliation. Psychoanalysis is a piece of the work of conciliation with one's own origins. The important ability to be implacable, attached to the wrong place in the neurotic unforgivingness toward the parents, has been freed for aspects of life where it can be used for efforts directed toward social change, the changing of conditions that cause avoidable suffering to countless human beings. The longtime impassable road of affection toward my parents, based on humor, has been re-opened. Simultaneously, there has been an increase in my ability to deny approval to persons and relationships that the latter had previously received under pressure caused by fear or habit.

The conditions in which my parents had to raise me and my siblings were hard, and they had practically no help in coping with these conditions, much less any help in terms of understanding. They themselves had never really been understood by their own parents. They were trained in obedience and sacrifice, and they did sacrifice their lives to their children, perhaps not having any choice in the matter. It is depressing to hate one's parents not because they were evil, but because they were not 'great' or successful. Fortunately this kind of hatred is most easily resolved in gratitude as soon as the connections are revealed. Without their sacrifices, I would not have gone anywhere. Both parents have read the manuscript, reacting with mortification and grief, and yet, after an understandable period of hesitation, they have agreed to its publication. Truly, I have reason to be grateful.

On rereading the manuscript, I found myself bothered by the language in many places. There are purple passages, sections full of egocentric coquetry, then again portions of the text in which the child or fairytale talk of analysis, or of the analyst, becomes cloying and obfuscating. Yet irony, its extent and function, seems the most apparent trait: as a means of resistance, it spreads over certain experiences, distancing and miming superiority, because I was unable to express these experiences in another, authentic or appropriate language. It seems particularly embarrassing in places where omnipotence and exaggerated self-esteem—out of the hothouse climate of transference—become apparent in grammar and vocabulary, where the narrating subject, due to excessive attention through the analytical perspective, mounts a high horse: as our gestures become expansive and theatrical in the early stages of intoxication, so does pomposity infiltrate into the subject's self-description; he has temporarily lost his everyday sense of proportion as scrutiny under the microscope makes him seem 'special' to himself. Depression and narcissistic disturbance were the components of my neurosis. For the second one, language is a suitable and revealing vehicle, and that is where a feeling of shame appears most justified.

October, 1972

The Report

Part I

Written Christmastime, 1971

It is a fairly solemn moment when you first embark on an experiment whose outcome is totally unknown. It could well be that I find myself, after a few days or weeks, confronted with fragments of a confession so poor that I can only set them aside in shame. That could well be the result of the attempt to describe processes that turn deeply internal matter inside out, and normally and rightly, take place under the protection of secure confidentiality.

Every attempt to describe or to circumscribe the experience of one's own on-going psychoanalysis will first of all meet with the analyst's familiar query: "What associations does that call up in you?" or: "What do you think that means?" These questions do not even have to emanate from the mouth of the patient analyst behind the couch. They have become internalized and are appropriate in the course of enterprise that suddenly wants to use the entire course of an analysis as its subject. The question about the legitimacy of the attempt will certainly not be silenced, but is bound to reappear at each successive level of intimate revelation. Here I can only deal with it briefly. It is a question that can be solved only by means of an analytical attitude in the very act of writing. First of all, a couple of catchwords: the main accusation will be one of exhibitionism. Colleagues directed it against me years ago at a conference when I tried to contribute something arising out of an episode of my analysis to the subject under discussion—the relationship between teacher-analysts and their students. It seemed to me then that the description of particular episodes or phases of the learning analysis might provide a wealth of scientific material for discoveries in the realm of psychoanalysis or of psychoanalytical education. When all is said and done, one's own learning analysis provides the base for one's professional tool kit, with which one then tries to aid other persons suffering from psychic illness. I realized immediately that I had touched upon a taboo: he who talks about his own analysis is *acting out*, and that is a bad thing to do. It is permissible only in patients whom one observes from an analytical distance: they are the sick ones who hope that we can help them. The accusation of "acting out" frightens the young analysts to the point of gooseflesh, striking, as it does, at their own deep doubts about their analytical competence. In patients, acting out is regrettable but normal: it provides material for new interpretations, and it is to be followed by remembering and working through. In the case of analysts, it is regarded as "sinful," certainly not without cause if it is taken to mean that one acts out of instinctive pressure without knowing what it is one is doing.

Thus, I have to deal with the accusation of acting out. That it occurs to me first demonstrates how wakeful and irritable the psychoanalytical, quasi-institutional superego is. I might even call it only partially internalized: it presents itself in externalized form as the image of the faces on the wagging heads of a few stern colleagues and psychoanalytical ancestors. Here, the first commandment is: Do not talk about your own analysis or you will be punished with possibly painful interpretations. It is not a senseless commandment. One who cannot bear to digest quietly the feelings and insights gained in psychoanalytical sessions will not be able to gain analytical 'weight.' The revivified early emotions will deliquesce even before the weakened ego can get hold of them and learn how to use them. On the third one of my three previous futile attempts to undergo psychoanalysis, I did destroy the possibility of help by acting out. After each session, I reported on it to an acquaintance who had an extremely ambivalent attitude toward this process. I became a spectator of my own analysis, a gossip even, and paid for it by the painful premature termination of it. In the course of the analysis that I am about to describe, I was not a spectator but an experiencer. I soon abandoned the attempt to jot down the occasional catchword, although the wish or thought to describe the experiences which arose a couple of months after the beginning of the treatment, despite fluctuations in intensity, never quite disappeared. It also survived all the analytical sessions that were devoted to the interpretation of this very wish. Some of these interpretations will most probably become evident in the following.

The first notion, during a session, as to why I wanted to write about the analysis: "I want to create a memorial for you." The analyst's counter-notion: "But that would mean that I am dead." One could of course contemplate that brief exchange for hours. Those in the know will instantly recognize the tangled thicket of conscious and unconscious motivations. The analyst was referring to the coming-to-terms with paternal authority and also the ambivalence in which that coming-to-terms was then taking place, and he gave a classical interpretation: "Death wishes." This was the beginning of prolonged mutual efforts to understand this attempt at a description. We discovered not only death wishes, but also many "life wishes", i.e., wishes to broadcast what he had achieved with me, and to praise him. This relates (I can only hint at it now) among other things to the fact that he does not, as it were, know how to write and is so emphatically private in the practice of his métier, to which I owe a great deal, that it often caused me pain, as it then seemed important to me that even my father "in science" be great. I have outgrown that; another thing I have to thank him for.

Of all the motivations, that of gratitude survived all analytical interpretations with the least damage. It is the one to which I commit myself even now as I am writing, regarding it as the main motive, although I realize how much exhibitionism there still is in play, and perhaps, first of all, pride in being of a line of descent of which, at long last, one does not feel ashamed.

In this case, gratitude is a quite specific occasion: this analysis proved to be an act of psychic life-saving. Who can say whether I might have committed suicide at some time: but during and after the second attempt to undergo psychoanalysis, I frequently visited a certain spot by the railroad tracks or, at night, a high bridge across a river that was notorious as a spot for noiseless suicides. But even if I did not do so, it was a fairly insufferable life I was leading under the label "depressive-narcissistic character neurosis".

The first attempt at analysis did not, by the way, founder, but I had to interrupt it, being compelled by ulterior reasons to move to another city, while fully intending to continue analysis there. The other two attempts were downright failures. One I terminated myself; the other one was terminated by the analyst. After them, I felt like a two-time loser, not only quasi-unfit to live, although this was a fairly well camouflaged aspect, but also threatened by the feeling that I was incapable of being healed. Whatever empathy may have entered into my work with prison inmates, it was not least due to my sense of being as much of an outcast as they were. The identification with their asocial situation provided me with a means for survival.

These hints are intended to clarify why I experienced my analysis as a successful life-saving operation for my soul. And there was yet another circumstance, minor but of great importance: it has to do with a characteristic of my analyst's that belongs to the great area of the relationship between psychoanalytical technique and humanity. At the psychoanalytical institute to which he belonged, it was the rule in those days that the diagnostic interview and the test results were discussed in the so-called "ambulance conference". This conference could be called the third diagnostic step, after interview and tests: by means of the therapists' spontaneous ideas and reactions to the anonymously presented case history, it contributes essential material to aid in the clarification of diagnosis and proposal of treatment. Having subsequently been a member of this conference many times, I am aware of the function, value and sense of responsibility of the gathering. At the time of my introduction to the institute—or, more exactly, of my shipwreck at its shore—I still saw it as a gathering of judges who were supposed to pronounce a definitive verdict on me. Their opinion was that my analyst, who had conducted my interview, should urge me to re-commence the course of analysis with the second analyst that I had broken off. I experienced this as condemnation. At that time, nothing would have moved me to go back. (Today, this is a cordial relationship.) I would have understood the verdict as confirmation of the idea that no psychoanalyst would have been able to help me and that I was "cast out" once and for all. As the conference minutes put it, laconically: "The patient is full of narcissistic fantasies about his own intrapsychic processes, and his ego is under high pressure. He has no genuine suppression mechanisms, his forms of defence are still, as it were, primeval. We expect there to be considerable difficulty in finding a mode of transference . . . back to Dr. Z., or, patient should not be accepted here. Assume very difficult, almost borderline kind of therapy." However, something must have occurred between the interviewer and me that caused him to adopt me, internally, against the decision of the conference. He did not have an open slot for me, so that I had to wait a year, a year of one-hour therapy. This adoption was not a rationally comprehensible experience. It appeared to me as a deliverance and became the cornerstone of a relationship which I came to describe, after a few years of analysis, by the term "inviolable". *He* is even to this day, after the naturally indispensable parents, the only person who has become psychically indispensable to me. This does not mean that I shall always need him: on the contrary, the end of analysis is drawing close. But the degree of my dependency on him is demarcated by the extent of supportive functions he has provided for me.

Another reason for *Years of Apprenticeship on the Couch* as the title of this attempted description: since I started my own therapeutic work with patients, I have become aware of the analyst's image continuing to be active through me. Sometimes in the course of an analytical hour with my patients, I notice how I am holding back or re-formulating an interpretation, whenever my own part in the analytical work wants to disappear for a moment behind my helpful memory of him. Yet I certainly don't want to copy him; he would not approve of that at all. Nevertheless, it is as if he were sitting behind me, my guardian angel, in those analyses and therapies I am now conducting myself.

The dependency on the analyst can be painful and humiliating at times. Whenever an analysis fails, it is traumatic. I, too, have raged against this dependency, against the infantilization, against the turning of one's life into a medium: that is to say, there are phases in analysis in which no action can be entirely comprehended without interpretive reference back to the status of the transference. For friends and relatives who cannot enter into this intimacy while experiencing its results, this is often painful. At the end of such a crisis of protest against the many umbilical cords that joined me to him, when I reproached him that I only dealt with the feelings of a female friend so helplessly because I was overly dependent on him, he said: "I know how difficult it can be for partners of analysands: many of them have thought about joining up with other fellow-sufferers to start an association of persons indirectly damaged by psychoanalysis."

For outsiders it is at times incomprehensible that it could be possible for a person to return to a couch, day by day, for years, behind which sits another person whom one does not know and to whom there are by and large no connections in real life. Yet, although I sometimes foamed with rage at his being built into my everyday life so solidly and at times gigantically, I have kept going to him, fairly regularly, even continuously, whenever I did not have to travel for professional reasons. Only recently, a couple of days before he went away on his Christmas vacation, and for the first time in almost four years of analysis, I simply forgot a session. It was not difficult to find the reason: I was afraid that the session might uncover an interpretation of my longstanding plan to use the vacation for writing the report that would, after all, make this writing impossible. Yet it was then possible to cast a much better light on the significances of this report.

Thus, I find myself writing without feeling that there is a conflict between him and me. It is obvious that my motives have bearing on *his* personal interests as well. It is true that I am not describing him, his real person, but psychoanalytically speaking his image in myself, the psychic representation—i.e., what I was able to perceive and receive. Nevertheless, this implies an imposition, almost an act of journalistic violence, against which he is helpless but for being able to demonstrate my motives to me. That again raises the question whether I want to persist, in view of all these meanings of my action. There is no doubt whatsoever that an irresistible urge to autonomy plays a part in it. True, I have paid him, and mostly out of my own pocket, but that has been merely my contribution to his social self-preservation. On another level, the writing may also have as its intention a lightening of the load of gratitude. One more thing that may relate: the knowledge of how many psychically ailing people there are, and how many among them are unable to find their therapist. It would be easy to say that those favored by chance would do better to keep their mouths shut. But silence does not diminish that sense of guilt which remains when one has participated in something inaccessible to the many and thus a privilege even when it cannot succeed without one's own engaged energies.

Whenever the psychoanalytical institute finds that it cannot cope with the number of people looking for help—and this has been the case for years—it directs them by means of a list of addresses to therapists living in the area. More than once a week I had the dualistic experience of lying on the couch and hearing my analyst tell some unknown patient on the telephone: "I am sorry, but I don't have a free slot." And, after a brief pause during which the stranger said something: "In two years at the earliest, but even that's unlikely." Sometimes I felt like a survivor in a small boat seeing countless others drifting in the water after a shipwreck.

The selection of those who do find a place functions in a strange way. They need endurance, faith, a certain ability to describe their ailment, a tolerance for frustration that is finally irrational but can nevertheless be categorized as "prognostically favorable" since it has to do with the motivation necessary for the analytical process. The opponents of psychoanalysis find this easy proof for the irrational character of the therapeutic event and even of its preparatory waiting period. Psychoanalytically, one might reply: analysis finds its starting point in exactly that glimmer of hope during the often long, patient wait, as it found its starting point in me, in an irrational hope with a strong admixture of desperation. However, I do not want this understood as some kind of justification for the present situation of therapeutic availability for many psychologically sick people. It is embarrassing to the therapist who has to keep on turning people away, and humiliating to the pleading patient. One would have to be a crypto-Darwinist to believe in a self-regulating supply and demand.

But that is a digression from my modest attempt to legitimize the book. I have mentioned the gratitude, the urge to autonomy, the sense of being the silent therapist's deputy as a writer. I saw myself as the subject, object and witness of a process that has deeply affected my life possibilities. In the meantime, I have started a practice as an analyst myself, and thus I am also describing the technique of treatment from the patient's point of view. There are a number of analysis reports by patients. These are psychoanalytically illuminated autobiographies that essentially present the contents of the early life, rediscovered in analysis, but not the road to that illumination. Examples are John Night's *Successful Psychoanalysis* or the *Journal d'une psychoanalyse* by Paul Diel. As far as possible, this book should not become a psychoanalytically illuminated autobiography. The emphasis should rather be on the decription of psychoanalysis as a process that can be experienced and technically described, thus centering on the craft aspect of it. The foremost question is: how does psychoanalysis work? Concrete autobiographical details serve only to clarify the pathological profile or the process of transference. My concrete past is uninteresting. I am not one of those contemporaries whose mere autobiography is important. A motive comparable to those of the two authors mentioned is perhaps this one: at the beginning stands the amazement at the experience. As I wanted to learn the craft of psychoanalysis myself, I paid close attention to the man behind the couch, to comprehend his practice of it.

I do not have many clear memories of the first year in one-hour therapy. It was a kind of first-aid to curb depression and to raise slowly my hopes of possible healing. Putting it another way, it served to prepare me for analysis and analytical regression. Towards the end of the year, I remember, I frequently cast longing looks toward the couch. I was overwhelmed by an almost irresistible urge to subside—into the arms of my psychoanalyst, of course, and as that was not possible, onto the couch. At times I felt as if I could not hold myself upright in that chair any longer, and it became obvious to both of us that it was getting to be time to allow layers to rise from the unconscious. In retrospect, I have to admit that he "managed" the surely difficult transition from chair to couch exceptionally well. As far as I can tell, no difficulties arose out of these quasi-fetal early days of sit-up analysis. Admittedly, a number of analysts are apt to regard this changeover as a blemish. I believe, though, that it meant a great deal in the diminution of my by that time boundless suspicion of all analysts, that I was able to scrutinize once a week not only his voice, but also his face, although I never succeeded in looking at him for long; very soon I found myself looking at the floor again. In his room there were, in addition to the comfortable armchair behind the couch, two other chairs, one upholstered and the other Spartan, hard. As if there had been no question about it, I at first took the hard chair that stood in my place in the room. After a few weeks, when he left the room for a moment at the beginning of the session, I switched the chairs, taking the upholstered one, not because I wanted that to be the definitive distribution, but because I tried to counteract a feeling of humiliation. He was quite surprised and told me no patient had ever thought of doing that. I don't remember how exactly we then interpreted the event. In retrospect, it appears to me to have been an unconscious manifestation of a desire for equality of rank, initially kept secret, and from the confused patient's view, an even arrogant desire. As far as I know, the event played no direct part in later events (although there were many later variations) except for a slight sense of surprise in me that he found the exchange of chairs rather strange, although he was so carefully concerned with the good of my soul. It is certainly no accident that I remember this incident. As a depressive, one frequently goes about wearing a mask of obedient humility, and behind it lurk all the unfulfilled demands of childhood. The degree to which one feels hurt marks an important moment in the course of the sickness. At a previous job, my vulnerability had earned me the apposite nickname of "Little Mimosa".

My rearrangement of the chairs also constituted a trusting offer, a premeditated symptom. At that moment, though, my main impression was that he was stunned for a moment to the point of being speechless. The knowledgeable will have already noticed that this was the first time a full-fledged infantile megalomania gave off a clear signal in this therapy. In what follows, that megalomania will present itself in its full dragon splendor: but it is possible to reveal in advance that it became halfway domesticated during those four years, as a kind of pet finding its nourishment no longer in the flesh of fellow humans or excessive fantasies but in solid work. One day, not too many weeks after the start of therapy, I had to get up to urinate before five minutes had passed. I thought quite innocently that I could do so: at the time I really believed, still, that it was possible to go out to pee during a psychoanalytical session without attaching any deeper significance to it. Well, I learnt otherwise. The unconscious often expresses itself in the most trivial gesture. Curiously enough I now remember nothing but minor conflict situations while writing this, because the following was undoubtedly one whose tracks extend throughout the analysis to this day, like those of megalomania. Its detailed explanation will have to wait until later. In any case, I returned from the toilet in all my assumed innocence, babbling something like "Hadn't been on the pot for a while" and "Forgot to go before the session" and similar psychoanalytical tyro stuff, blatant rationalizations of the kind that make one shake one's head six months later when remembering. And right there and then, the good fellow launched into careful interpretations: he said he had noticed that I had left the door open, as if to avoid interrupting contact, and perhaps even in the unconscious hope that he might possibly follow me to the john. As I stared at him in disbelief, he asked me why I had come back with my fly open. I felt my ears turning red, my forehead becoming dewy and then wet with perspiration.

To be frank about it, that interpretive attack did not sit too well with me then. One might say that the man had too high an opinion of my tolerance, and not without cause. As far as theory and personal experience with analysts went, I already was quite smart, not to say shrewd. Theoretically I would have regarded the entire incident as one of the more lighthearted psychoanalytical jokes. But as I see things today, I was then lying (no, sitting) down in the first delights of infant love, in which it is quite acceptable to offer one's little tail up to the ministrations of dear mommy. Yet at the same time I was a young man hideously afraid of homosexuality, and quite probably considerably infatuated with my savior. With a spasm of negation and re-repression I decided the thing was an accident and returned to the order of the day, depressive complaining. The incident remained buried for a long time, resurfacing only a short time ago, what is more, after an analytical session in which the attempt was to clarify why I experience difficulty in the working out of my homosexual tendencies. It did, however, have repercussions, as I realize right now: without my noticing it, it strengthened my seduction hypothesis in the unconscious. That meant, although this is a jump ahead, that for a long time I was so afraid of my own homosexual attraction to the analyst that my own perception, time and again, was of attempts on *his* part to seduce me. I stuck to that, almost painfully, and the daring analytical grasp of my obvious 'present' in a situation where the transference state still was somewhat unclear did no doubt reinforce that insistence. Curiously enough, there were, in this area of homosexuality, other minute incidents that helped slow down the process of working out. Being throttled by fear, the analysand grasps at every straw that promises delay.

At this point, I naturally ask myself why I start off with analytical episodes that might give rise to the impression that my analyst committed serious mistakes. Thus, I listen to my insides for a while, in the accustomed manner, switch off the typewriter, meditate, come up with this as motivation: don't make the only-too-easy impression of exaggerated evaluation of the love object, of immature idealization; demonstrate your ability to keep a critical distance; do not give the enemies of the craft any ammunition or arguments that propose, for instance, that the whole thing is possible only if you are a starry-eyed believer. On the other hand I realize how tenaciously those episodes have stuck to my memory, and this must be due to a tendency *against* idealization, a care not to overestimate or to fall in love with the analyst to the degree that I had done during the third futile attempt. Overall, the possibility of writing something about this analysis appears to be connected to the situation of the "burnt child" who remains, in a part of himself, a spectator after all—more precisely: one who has posted a lookout, as it were, under orders to give quicker warning than before. Thus, it is possible that I wanted to curb my still-existing tendency to love and admire precipitously by keeping my eyes wide open for small flaws. Under these conditions, many aspects of the analysis certainly proceeded more slowly and strenuously, with greater resistance, than they would have had I met this artist of empathy sooner and in a less preoccupied state. This was perhaps paralleled by that discovery of the human being in back of the therapist's analytical technique that mostly remains shadowy and sketchy. I do not want to advise any patient to aim for that. It may cause fundamental disturbances in the analysis. I did it against my will, probably self-defense, trying to ward off the possibility of another crash. And I experienced it as a triumph—not a negative, self-assertive one, but rather as a form of recognition, when he once told me that I had perceived a great deal about him and his singularities without his ever having discussed them with me. Indeed, there is no other human being whom I have studied as intensively as him. In the beginning, this study served to test his reliability, and later it turned into an interest in his strengths and weaknesses and, in part, his emotional life. What I had experienced as disappointment at first then became transmuted into sympathy. The discovery of his emotional world was important because I had not known, as a child, whether adults *had* any emotions except for those manifested in extreme situations.

There has stuck in my memory another episode of therapy, the full implications of which were similarly unknown until later. During a session I was sitting there, facing him, when I suddenly felt stopped, as if the brakes had been slammed on. He said: "I notice that you are running your fingertips across the edge of the table, ever so carefully." This made a strong impression. I saw myself understood as well as found out. I was astonished by his perception and by the degree of empathy it demonstrated. While I had not been conscious of my finger game, it did at that moment represent a significant activity: it tied up a part of my attention and my feelings, it was a recourse to, even a clutching at, my own fingertips. The experience of being found out most probably had to do with the fact that a form of resistance or reaction had suddenly become evident, possibly also with my inability to deal with my own strong emotions. He summed it up in one brief sentence: "Sensations instead of feelings."

Such experiences had a twofold effect. They reinforced the feeling of security. They contained loving revelations of hidden processes, and thus they made me shed a little piece of my fear each time. Secondly, they furthered my sense of admiration. There were times when I literally gulped with surprise. And then, once in a while, something strange happened to this pseudo-coldblooded intellectual: I had to muster all my strength to keep from embracing him. That is not a very comfortable situation. Two grownup men sit facing each other, and one of them experiences a desire to embrace the other in what is almost a fit of emotion. This gave rise to an entirely different kind of fear. It is one of the peculiarities of psychoanalysis that the dissolution of fear on one level can mobilize it on the next as soon as repressed matter starts moving again there.

During the year of initial therapy and even a few months into the proper analysis, I had to travel to the sessions for an hour by train or automobile. I remember some of the trips on the train. There I was sitting in the open compartments of an express train, people talking and laughing, and for me all that was only half-real. Clumsily, I can sum up my feelings like this: you poor people sit there unsuspecting in your everyday reality and don't even notice that there is one among you who is on his way to therapy with Dr. X! I felt like one elect who carried a secret with him. While writing this, I can't help noticing that "elect" sounds pretty highflown, not to say bombastic—yet it would be of no use for me to deny the emotional states I experienced at that time. Cognoscenti will not be surprised about that. They will have noticed some time ago that things did not look bad for me at all in prognostic terms, although it would be a mistake to equate "prognostically positive" with "simple analysis". It was "prognostically positive" specifically for an analyst like him. I believe he saw that himself: he was able to recognize, by means of all kinds of symptoms, that the analytical fish-hook had taken a deep hold, in the cardiac muscle, as it were. This would also serve to explain why he never wavered in his patience and resolution when I tortured him with doubts, criticism, deprecation, and accusations to the effect that there was no recognizable progress. And this is an essential point: *he* never lost faith in me, not even when I myself thought that all was lost. Those were the times I went to the session feeling like an idiot who goes on acting a part in some absurd play because he cannot think of anything better to do, and because he cannot deal with the scandalous fact that the analyst awaits him with consistent friendliness, perhaps even lets him know that he has noticed that things are going worse now exactly because hatred and rage and suspicion are struggling to gain the upper hand.

Something else comes to mind. On one occasion I mistook the date or missed the train, did not, in any case, make it to the session. The following week I was overcome by my urge to independence: I made up my mind to decide and stick to a certain date for my next session, hoping that *he* would then agree to this change. I called him, asking him for a new date, but he did not comply: gently but firmly he urged me to wait until the following week. It took me quite a while to get over that. Through defiance and frivolity I had managed to arrange a break of three weeks, with all the painful alienation that such a break entails. I then realized that *I* was responsible for the regularity of the sessions, and that I had to get over my anger over the extent of coercion that lay in the fact of *his* schedule. One could obviously call this an act of submission, but that may well be the wrong term. It has to be a matter of organization, after all. Thus, I was slowly able to deal with his hardness, no longer interpreting it as meanness but as an appeal to my reliability, comparable to his own, which was greater than any I had experienced in another person. Later, by the way, he was quite accommodating when I was unable to attend certain sessions, and took great pains to rearrange the schedule when I was truly under pressure. On the other hand, he sometimes allowed me the choice between an analytical session and some other appointment of mine. He did, in other words, basically leave me to judge for myself on the value I assigned to the regularity of the sessions. The rule that I had to pay for the session even when I did not show up, except in case of illness, was also conducive to discipline.

I would now like to proceed from the initial therapy to the analysis, with the obvious reservation that important aspects of the former will be incorporated as they occur to me. As regards the analysis, I should perhaps discuss the megalomania once more, since it represents the counterpart to depression. After a few weeks of analysis, i.e., daily sessions in the reclining position, I once said, feeling sated, omnipotently comfortable, and in the patronizing and grandpaternal tone I tend to adopt in such moods: "Well, well, Dr. X., I certainly think that you are a pretty good analyst. But I'll force you to become a *very* good analyst." He responded to these programmatic sentences with a resounding burst of laughter—the first time he did so, I believe, though by no means the last. Yet I did not feel put down by his laughter, I felt understood. Besides, he repeatedly let me know in the course of the long analysis that he had indeed learnt a great deal, through me and from me: nor was this meant to be flattering in the least, but rather indicated almost collegial recognition. That, in any case, is how I perceived it in the later years. At first it was more like a present, a delicate adjustment of my sense of my own value. The programmatic content of that statement was, of course, that I was not willing to drop below a certain analytical level on this, my fourth, attempt at analysis. To translate the whole thing into the infantile lingo of which he is a master, partly through association with his own children, partly because he has spent a long time working as a physician in children's clinics, the message would simply be: If you don't help me to pee the highest and longest arc, I'll be cross with you.

At times, when the dragon of omnipotence lay limp on the ground, my experience of things was naturally quite different. I can provide an immediate example for this, although I do not know which phase it belongs to. His couch was adjustable at the head: I had gotten used to an intermediate position, with the bars below the couch in the first or second slot, and a pillow under my head. One day I arrived at a time different from the usual, and some idiot of a fellow patient who had preceded me, evidently the owner of a warped neck, had readjusted the couch and its elevation, and the pillow too was missing. Thus, I had to lie down in a perfectly horizontal position, and before I knew it, I was in a state of panic. Things began to turn in my head. It occurred to me that I was lying on the bed of a dump truck and that it was slowly rising, the bed being the couch, my legs slowly rising, higher and higher. Soon I would tumble backwards into his lap. In a state of uninhibited projection, I regarded this as some perfidious scenario created by the devil, with whom I often believed the analyst to be in cahoots, and started to groan. Only when he asked me what the matter was did I succeed in finding words to describe the disquieting event. Yet my resistance was still so strong that I found it immensely difficult fully to realize the experience as a scenario of my own: it was not *I* who yearned to be secure in his lap, it was an infernal machine that had to catapult me there against my will. After that, I took care to build a dam against him, out of pillows, until I became more forward again and, full of fearful titillation, started experimenting again with the slanted plane. Once again, I experienced mild vertigo, but I endured it without calling for pillows or adjusting the couch frame. This time, the interpretive image that occurred to me came from another region. I remembered the picture of the hole the anteater digs and felt like the insect that irrevocably slides down to the bottom and into the voracious beast's claws, no matter how energetically it struggles at the rim. Besides other contents, this image already heralded a level of transference that I really dared approach only in the fourth year of analysis—the one on which father or mother appear as Moloch devouring his children. In retrospect I find it surprising how long I was able to postpone that level after the anteater image had given such a direct pointer. It seems this was not evident to the analyst either, and again, for good reasons, since we were at the time engaged in the battle against my fears of physical proximity to a male and thus remained, collectively or at least in part, on a less archaic level of interpretation.

Later, it bothered me less and less to lie relatively flat on my back, even though it always caused some malaise. In the new offices my analyst moved into after a while, there was a big pile of cushions on the couch, and thus it was possible to accomplish unobtrusive individual "dosage". Yet it was possible to deduce something from the height of the cushion mountain as to the height of the dam my fellow patients had to build against the anteater's attraction. Since I had a good eye for such things, due to a never-ending, though gradually transformed, sibling rivalry, I was later able to console myself with patronizing remarks about the suckling babes and creepy-crawlies who were new to his practice and obviously still very much afraid of the anteater.

I see how difficult it becomes to make selections from the

torrent of notions and memories. Now I could follow up the associations with sibling rivalry and fellow patients, quite certainly losing my way in the affects and images. The question arises: what does a newborn know about his siblings? In the analysis, I think, I made a jump forward to those times when the infant has already begun to carry the dagger in his pants, and to grab ahold of it once in a while. Strangely enough, I have no recollections whatsoever from my first year as regards sibling rivalry. That is not really surprising, however, because I was then the youngest one, and as we know, the youngest always enjoy a good life. I hope that I made good use of it.

However, here comes a memory right out of the playpen—yet endowed with the imaginative powers of one at least twelve months old: indeed, it was the first affective perception of a rival on the couch. "The old lady", if I may call my analytical father that for the purposes of this phase of transference, had arrived late at the beginning of the day (as he commuted to his office, this happened sometimes) and had therefore spent a few minutes longer with my predecessor on the couch. In view of my impetuous needs, this seemed rather incomprehensible to me and was soon converted into a painful disappointment in mother and a first, tentative and quasi pre-Oedipal experience of her perfidy. I cannot remember if I perceived the fellow before me as a person at all, but as soon as I lay down on the couch, I had the notion that I was lying in a warm puddle of urine. This was so unpleasant that I went into the most bizarre contortions in order to stay close to the edge of the bed, and to spare most of my posterior surface from the sensation of sticky wetness. It goes without saying that I complained and blasphemed a lot, but to no avail. He was able to justify himself on the basis of a traffic emergency, and it was not, in any case, possible to deny the existence of siblings any longer. My perception of them did, however, occur accompanied with qualities of feeling customary among infants. This was not in the least accidental: as a depressive type, I had been a real pro bedwetter, long before puberty. Thus, urine was a medium of communication with which I was quite familiar. The person to whom I attributed the urine, on the grounds of some residual warmth on the couch surface, became my first younger sibling in analysis, and if one chooses to reverse the projection, it could well be that my feeling was a cover-up for the wish to drown him in my own urine.

When I was all of eighteen months old on the couch, we arrived, as the progression of the year cannot be halted even by infantile magic, at the analyst's second summer vacation. At that time I felt quite big enough for my boots and, although I still had not much to do with the official guild of analysts, travelled brazenly to the world congress of psychoanalysts in Rome, as if to satisfy my curiosity about the secrets of a worldwide congregation of parents, and then to report on them in the newspaper for the benefit of other Nosey Parkers. At that time, the first Americans had either landed on the moon or orbited it—in any case, human beings had engaged in rather complicated adventures of meeting and finding each other again in outer space. I imagined the return from vacation and the rendezvous with the analyst in terms of space travel and a so-called splashdown, Monday morning at nine o'clock on the couch. I had encountered and greeted him briefly among the crowds in Rome. As agreed, there had been a portion of airless "outer space" between us, unpleasant to the nostrils, beastly cold and hurtful. This made the spot landing, four weeks later, all the more important: I imagined him the aircraft carrier. I came down on the dot, brake parachutes wide open so as not to crash into him in damagingly stormy fashion, and what happened? The secretary informed me that I would have to wait a little longer, sorry, but Dr. X was busy with an emergency case. I saw the small red lamp lit above his door, which meant: stop, don't come in, I am already giving suck to somebody. This is putting it with pre-Oedipal restraint. Later, whenever I had to wait, that little red light became a true whore's beacon, symbol of treason, serial therapy, assembly line treatment, psychic prostitution, etc. etc. Well, the light was on, and the aircraft carrier and an emergency case were behind that door: I had to splash down on a hard wooden chair in the anteroom. After fifteen minutes, he emerged in the company of an elderly woman who was presumably suffering from a neurotic case of blindness and whom I would surely have pitied under other circumstances. At that time, I only recognized her as the old witch of the fairytale. After a while of mute sulking on the couch I talked about the image of landing and retrieval of the Apollo or Gemini capsule. "Do you understand, after orbiting moon and earth, I come floating down to you, exactly on course and on time, and expect you riding here at anchor, waiting for me. But what do you do, instead of catching me, beaming with joy? You are busy rescuing a shipwrecked fishing yawl."

Naturally, I have to ask myself why such matters have remained in my memory in such exact verbal detail. The question opens up a variety of possible interpretations. As a man of letters, I am, anyway, foolishly preoccupied with linguistic structures. Yet the memories are also due to the fact that the verbal inventions represent an intensive wooing of the analyst. It was possible my fear of not being loved enough occasionally spurred me on to entertaining peak performances. These were, of course, interpreted, but that was only partially helpful. Besides, that wooing verbal eroticism occurred at a time when there was much discussion of my real or feared bad smell, of the penetrating stench of urine that accompanied me throughout childhood, and of the stink of sweat that I thought I was wearing like a cloak, since I did sweat a lot, and sweated more the more afraid I was, couldn't work, felt under pressure, suffered from guilt feelings: it was verbal perfume, one might say, laboriously concocted in order to obliterate my own stench. It was difficult for me even to raise the subject. One day I felt: it stinks to high heaven. I was sweaty, unwashed, unshaven, half derelict. Memories like the following went through my head: in the daytime, I rarely peed my pants, and if I did, then only in church (this is a pointer to the ecclesiogenic part of my neurosis: both my grandfathers were clergymen). Or: I am bouncing around on the parental bed, freshly made by my mother, take a crap on the fresh bedsheet and have such a good time enjoying the impressive optical aspect of the result until I get whacked. In short, I am surrounded by images of urethral and anal painfulness and feel utterly shitty, while still being just about able to communicate it. Then comes the voice from behind the couch: "Your unspoken question to me is really this: can you go on holding such a filthy and stinking child in your arms, or will you throw it away? But a good mother can go on holding a child in her arms even when it is covered in shit from head to toe." Then the solid layer of shit that I felt was enveloping me was pierced by a shudder of well-being, so that I had to laugh out loud. From then on, the stench slowly receded from me.

It is strange how little comes to mind from the first months of analysis. They were dedicated to the balancing-out of my depression. For instance, there was the important question whether I was able to talk at all. At times, it was impossible, it was too much of a strain to open the mouth, or it just did not seem worthwhile, in that state of dejection. Sometimes there was simply complaint, for hours and hours, almost whimpering, combined with immense shame over this prostrate inability to go on, this hopelessness. It could take on the appearance of physical illness: I just lay there, unable to move an arm or a leg. Perhaps I just have to wait until those memories return spontaneously. They won't let themselves be forced: the bad weekends: the feeling that only the momentarily dormant vein of analysis connected me to life: Friday, Saturday, Sunday, nothing but waiting for Monday morning. On occasion I sat in front of the telephone on Saturday or Sunday, leafing through my address book. Some acquaintances weren't home, some had other visitors, but most of them I did not even try to call. They would not have been capable of dealing with my condition, nor would I have been up to their notions of sociability. Or I did go and visit people I knew, but the feeling remained that the level of contact was the wrong one. These were the times of grasping sexuality, of quasi-intoxicated smooching and frantic fucking, of a flash-in-the-pan happiness that contained the urge to run away again soon, mere orgiastic sucking.

Nor does that characterize all the relationships, but the low points: a desperate unfaithfulness, because the greedily created proximity soon gave rise to fear again and could be dissolved only by means of flight. There are people who were *victims* of my neuroses; suffering that was caused, treason, aroused and then disappointed hopes, demolished relationships—that mixture of torturing and helping that causes wounds which may never heal again. I believe that among other things guilt feelings drove me to tell one partner after another to go into analysis themselves: I did not want them to be the prey of only *me* and my and their cumulative traumas. And I did not want them to fall into the void when it became obvious that there was no staying power to what I started over and over again in my addictive greed of relationship without being able to give it enduring form.

Remembering these things, I keep coming back to one image. One morning I arrived late for my session at the institute. I was sad and fearful, not least because of my tardiness, and *he* had left his room and walked down the hall to the window from which you can look down into the street. I came running round the corner, almost panicky with compounded weight of superego and self-condemnation and fear of loss of love and being late, saw him standing up there, smiling at me. Both my arms flew up in the air toward him. Only then did I see the other people in the street and let my arms fall to my sides again, but in my imagination I had thrown them around his neck, although I found it difficult to even express such things then.

It is certain that he could not agree to my sometimes almost blind search for affection, sexual relations, acknowledgment. But none of what my berserk conscience attributed to him, projected onto him in terms of condemnation, revulsion, rejection, loss of respect and affection, was true. Frequently I turned him, for weeks if not months, into the bad mother who did not feel I deserved anything, who sat there shaking her head. Next to the primitive feeling of safety when close to him, it was probably that cautious projection of my shattered superego onto him that filled out the initial period. I was a master of projection and perceived each twinge of my own conscience first as a wrinkling of his brow, a dimming of his gaze. At all times it was possible to conjure up a catastrophe in his regard, through some attitude of thought. When he arrived five minutes late, I was lost. After three minutes, I had given up on myself and needed deep sorrow, sulking, or rage in order to return to the surface. I suffered from an immense ability to be hurt at the slightest suspicion of rejection, of lovelessness, even just a diminution of his affection; likewise, from a gigantic susceptibility to my own hypertrophic melancholic's conscience, which at that time was entirely dependent on him. This liability to be hurt was possibly increased by the repeated suggestions emanating from my stern and sometimes even sadistic superego: all bad things that happen between him and you are entirely deserved, because you are evil. For months I lived in the fear that he was bound to recognize the uselessness, even depravity, of my character, and would then send me home with regrets.

The analysis was a protracted revision of the impossibility of accepting myself. Whoever has a theoretical interest can read up on it in Freud's article about melancholy. It is, in part, my own tale of woe, at least on that analytical level. In the times of being easily hurt, my readiness for misunderstanding became boundless. If he finished the session thirty seconds before time, or I just happened to think so, this became a sense of having been "thrown out", or else I fantasized that he was barely able to await the end of the session, to be rid of me at last. If he exchanged a few words with colleagues in the hall, he appeared to me as a finally revealed traitor who conducted demonstratively idiotic conversations in order to torture me. This was worst when he talked to women or girls: then I felt excluded, definitively and for all time. Speaking of the revision of this self-rejection, I remember a dream from the second attempt at analysis which finally turned into a painful daydream: A man has discovered a nest of young ravens, grabs them by the feet, and beats their heads against a tree trunk in order to kill them. This arose out of an actual former experience, but now it became a symbol for the way I was treating myself. Sometimes those young ravens turned into a child, especially during the time I was making a living by reporting on the great Auschwitz trial. During the trial, there was mention of such a method of infanticide in front of the crematoria, and in my dreams I always assigned the role of the killed child to myself. Slowly my self-hatred weakened. How this came to pass, I cannot say exactly. It must have to do with an amelioration of the superego, probably also with a lessening of an attendant hatred against my mother which I was almost unable to understand at a conscious level. That hatred burst into fresh flames during analysis, simply because it had become accessible again. Although I was no longer tempted to direct it against actual persons, it could happen that I took walks for many hours during which I was inwardly preoccupied with nothing but hating: the objects were the analyst and my mother, turn and turn about. Any small difficulty in actual life had the possibility of expanding into a catastrophe of rejection, culminating in endless tirades of revenge. I felt persecuted, rejected, beaten and battered, belched bile and fire, was shaken by hatred. The analyst could change from angel to devil and vice versa from one hour to the next. Later, he told me, apropos the characterization of that initial phase which with its ups and downs lasted at least eighteen months: "At that time you were offering me almost exclusively raw surfaces, and the gentlest touch was enough to trigger great pain." To my mind, that was an excellent résumé. For a year he concentrated, almost exclusively, on treating the wounds, a truly thankless endeavor, my condition having been complicated by my hatred against the other two unsuccessful analysts. On one hand, this helped make him appear in glorious contrast, at first, but confusion was very easy. Then I hated, in him, the entire profession, calling its members exploiters and sadists, torturers and elitists. How should a child know how long it takes even to lay bare the wounds? At the time, I often accused him of needing my pain for his own well-being. Many insults I regarded as consciously programmed, designed to keep me in a state of suffering. I was paranoid at an early stage, and as he was a monster, I myself grew boundlessly in my revenge fantasies in order to destroy him and his fellow practitioners one day. I developed a cold sarcasm, using it from time to time really to torture him. I certainly had sufficient schizoid powers of empathy to recognize when he let his guard down. His feelings were much friendlier than mine, and I directed my sarcasm against them, because I thought they were signs of weakness; I called him a kitschdigger, a rose garden lyricist, a sweet-talker for small children and old maiden aunts. I had armored myself against the invitation in his voice. When he developed interpretive images that were directly relevant to my condition, I let him fall—with a hearty ho-ho, as I believed—into the gutter of sentimentality.

But he endured it all because he knew that I was hurting myself far more than I was hurting him. Yet how furious I was when he told me that: "Above all, I see how you are torturing yourself and feel bound to destroy what is good." He was right, but I had to rage and destroy and satirize, to extinguish the emergent emotions, time and again. Everything appeared to me as dirty lies, traps designed to lure me back into early unhappiness, into a time when I, in order to deal with my hatred for the siblings and the psychic loss of my mother, dissected frogs and small fishes with splinters of glass. Here I remember one of his interpretations, although I do no longer know to which one of my verbal misdeeds it responded. He said, "Young children sometimes want to, or have to, find out if they can cause adults pain, because they want to know whether they themselves *are there* at all, whether they have any power. And you want to know, exactly, if it hurts." At times, cautiously, he permitted me to notice that I had scored a direct hit, whenever I had managed to destroy a bit of friendliness again, and was grateful when I was able to understand that without fear of retribution. That was not the case very often, as my guilt complex exaggerated everything about him that I did not like into acts of revenge. If, during a session, he talked less than usual, I experienced this as a devilish letting-me-stew-in-my-own-juices, although it actually was only an attempt to find out if I was able to take two or three steps by myself without getting encouragement every couple of minutes. "You're letting me flounder," I would then say, sometimes with impotent rage, sometimes in the full awareness of my misery. There also were times when it turned into a power struggle, and he needed, no doubt, a great deal of analytical acuity to find out how steep a dive I had just taken or how belligerent I was really feeling. Every analyst and every analysand knows the struggle for the first step or the first word, frequently even for the first noise uttered in a session, which is to determine who makes the first move in the direction of the other. Very often I needed that bridge, but many times things worked even when he remained silent long enough, even though I then experienced it as a minor humiliation and felt enraged. Yet, whenever he felt that I would not make it on my own, he always helped me. I well know that there are analysts who would rather bite off their tongues than come to the aid of their patients. I am sure they have their reasons, but I know with certainty that I would not have been able to stand it. As soon as Mom or Dad, depending on the transference situation, noticed that I was strong enough for the power struggle, the interpretation began, and—strictly speaking—naturally proved the futility of that struggle to me every time.

I want to relate, briefly, an episode that appears symbolic to me for a condition I would like to call post-depressive peace, as regained joy in play and in one's own growth, but also for a phase in which regression no longer was merely a conglomerate of a desire for fusion and a fear of being devoured. It happened one day that I noticed, a few minutes after the session had begun, how good I felt. I signaled this by means of a grunting sound, non-verbal, voluptuous, quite animal-like. In response, I heard him utter a similar sonorous grunt, deeper, confirmatory, an equally animal-like affirmation of mere presence. And now there ensued a dialogue of grunts, as when the mama sow and a single piglet lie in the sun, do not see each other, but want to communicate in *their* language, thus non-verbally to our crude ear, yet not without animal enjoyment of broad modulation: "Hello, are you there?" "Yes, I'm here, you too?" "Sure I am, you can hear it, can't you?" "What do you mean, I didn't hear anything, say it again!" And then they spend some time grunting back and forth, just because it is such a pleasure to be together and to measure the closeness of the other by the sounds and the brief echo intervals. One might say that this marked the end of depression as a chronic illness, although there were relapses, sometimes severe relapses. But I was, once again, able to lie in the sun and to combine proximity and distance better than before.

Certain episodes or analytical progressions have a similar and shared function as reinforcements of the relationship for therapist and patient alike. They are shared memories *in* the analysis to which one can refer, either to reassure oneself of the other's presence, or to clear up misunderstandings. Yet there are other key episodes that each one experiences by himself, or in which the depth of the experience differs. Naturally, the depth of experience is different anyway, simply because the analyst's emotional engagement has to remain measured and controlled, whereas, within limits, a loss of control on the patient's part is, indeed, a prerequisite for success. In any case, to him one such key experience seems to have been an episode that certainly had its significance for me, but did not have the same guiding importance for the entire analysis that he found in it. This relates, by the way, back again to the beginning of therapy. As I have said, I suffered from the anxiety of one who has been punished, or has failed repeatedly, and was under pressure to prove myself worthy of therapy while simultaneously dealing with the strongly resurgent traces of my hatred for the second analyst. There is, finally, a temptation in these cases to woo the new analyst by describing the previous one's shortcomings in a way that will be flattering to the new one—really a fairly complicated situation, in which I myself struggled to find an explanation for the failure of the second analysis. It had foundered on my hatred and my suspiciousness which I had no longer been able to keep in check. So I said, pleading for sympathy: "You know, when you have to deal with so much hatred as I had, in therapy, then you need to have a very good and loving relationship going on with it, and I just did not get that." This must have impressed him as a powerful appeal, and it became decisive for his "inner course". He kept referring back to that beginning, and one might say that the episode appealed to his maternal instinct. That sounds corny: yet I have not become, even after the successful analysis, a sentimentalist. The case is rather that I was gradually able to assimilate the analyst's vocabulary, even though I did not adapt it for my own use. That, again, is due to the fact that he, while being extremely literate and educated, when dealing with the patient's feelings and even with his own when he formulated them in an interpretive response, often became almost illiterate, verbally, and knew it and often apologized, quasi-prophylactically, for his "stammering" (as he once called it) when launching into a longer interpretive sequence. To get back to the subject: I wanted to say that this initial episode and his way of perceiving it became a foundation for the analysis. One might even call it an act of baptism in which he took on the full extent of his responsibility, his analytical, maternally tinged *paternity*.

His reliable *maternity* was likewise connected to an episode whose importance dawned on me only gradually, from his interpretations. The conversation in which the commencement of the one-hour therapy was agreed upon took place about a month before his four weeks of summer vacation. It would have been quite normal to postpone the beginning to a date after his return. Yet I must have felt a minute response of accommodation on his part because I proceeded to urge him to give me the first hour of therapy (or love) even before the vacation. Later, he told me that this had amounted to an act of impetuous and loving rape, and that he had noticed that I was not ready to allow any vagueness but wanted to establish what was what immediately, i.e., to define the proprietary relationship, in order to save him from the least little bit of temptation to become unfaithful to me once more during the vacation. After this analytical defloration I was able to endure the waiting period much better.

Perhaps I can use this context to make an observation as to the possible reasons for the failure of my second analysis. Theoretically speaking, one might say that it became unbearable for me and possibly even for the analyst because the ambivalence swung way over into hatred and the libidinous base gradually eroded away or was actively destroyed by me. One of my final utterances after those two years was: "Now I realize that I wanted to torture you." I believe that I had trapped myself in a masochistic triumph. My present analyst has provided a further explanation that illuminates many things. He himself realized it only when we encountered forms of positive idealization that were difficult to comprehend. He said: "It strikes me that what you experienced then was a case of negative idealization." This would mean that I distorted the second analyst in the direction of magnitude, even in transference, while providing him with mainly negative and dangerous qualities, best subsumed in the words "cold, unfeeling potency". In actuality, of course, there are hardly any reasons for that caricature. Yet I remember, immediately after this interpretation, my very first impression in the second analyst's room, which I had not hesitated to communicate to him: "You seem to me like a cool diplomat behind his boss desk." Seedlike, that statement already contained the end. As indicated before, present relations are cordial and collegial. At this point, I ask myself if it would not be better to leave all this unsaid, based as it is on a great deal of painful failure. But the breakdown of an analysis is painful by definition, and associated with disappointment, recriminations, complaints and hatred over a long period of time. With my present analyst I have dedicated much time and energy to the unraveling of that failure, and he has attended to the re-establishment of good relations to the other analyst with the same interpretive and even encouraging patience that he has mustered in many other endeavors. Thus, this represents an area of the success of this analysis and an object of my gratitude. Even among analysts there are rivalries, and the transfer of patients with whom one has had difficulties, much more so the taking-on of a patient who parted from another analyst with hatred, is no easy matter, touching as it does on the analyst's fantasies of greatness and his need for triumph. It is, so to speak, dirty analytical wash that one expects to encounter there, and all that causes confusing, if not overwhelming, emotions and fantasies in the child that the re-adopted, regressed patient then has become. In no case would the reworking of the failure to the point of reconciliation have been possible without a high degree of human integrity in the analyst and his reliable collegial loyalty to the former analyst, a loyalty which did not preclude temporary empathy with the accusing patient.

One of the fundamental problems of this attempt to describe a course of psychoanalytical treatment is unquestionably the doubt whether and how far it is possible to adopt an even halfway detached and distanced point of view toward one's own neurosis. Normally, we just live our neuroses, hardly knowing that we have any. The world in which one exists and the people with whom one lives appear in a neurotic coloration that is no longer recognized as coloration. I spent tortuous years before even guessing at the possibility that I might be suffering from anything like that, i.e., until I was able to look for help and to accept it. Before that, shame was predominant, the tendency to hide one's own difficulties, the desperate hope that it was merely a question of crises of maturation that would at some time resolve themselves. During my first couple of semesters as a student, I had already reached a point where I was ready to turn to a psychotherapist, but then I allowed the sarcasm directed against that guild by a teacher I admired to prevent me doing so, reinforcing the shame tendencies and at the same time radicalizing the attempt to transmute the neurosis into a form of existence with literary trappings. But there are certain degrees of depressivity and contact disturbance that restrict one's freedom to define one's own condition and its medico-psychological nomenclature, or even abolish it altogether. In my student digs I broke out in cold sweats of fear, in class I was overwhelmed by panic. There were days when I was able to go on reading in the library only if I went and masturbated from time to time. The frivolous consolation of an occasional fuck in the woods disappeared because of a temporary affliction with ejaculatio praecox. I do begin to feel uncertain as to the possibility of discussing one's neurosis the way one can talk about a case of t.b. or a heart valve defect. I am suddenly overcome by shame, and the question arises: *Am I not, after all, my neurosis?* Do I not draw a definitive image for the public, will I not become a marked man, if I admit to all that? In a discussion with friends, I have referred to this description as a medical experiment on myself.

By the enumeration of a few symptoms I wanted to indicate that I was no longer living the neurosis, but that it had begun to live me. It became stronger than I, and there were times when my life consisted merely of the attempt to alleviate it. It would be possible to say that the neurosis would have conquered or ruined me but for the fact that I decided after reaching a certain pain threshold to say: that's enough, now I'll just grin and bear them, the sense of not being able to cope, the label of psychological disturbance. Today, ten years later, it has become considerably easier to have a neurosis without being desperately ashamed about it.

In a certain sense, the analysis represents an objectification of the neurosis. Step by step it becomes activated, performed, as it were, in transference to the therapist: hundreds of hours of shared viewing of psychological x-ray pictures, some of them full-scale, some of microscopic detail. That creates detachment and a certain overview. *I am and am not my neurosis.* Slowly it is shed, not without leaving traces and scars; the psychoanalytical character image does not just fade away. I remain vulnerable to depression, and I have to go on struggling with the dragon of megalomania. I have to try to tame it. The pathological: the sense of suffering attacks, the depression extending over days and weeks—these have gone away, and when a depressive phase occurs I can trust it to be shorter, knowing that I have acquired a kind of interpretive power over it (and at the present moment, the analyst is still assisting me), even that I have become manageable. Thus I am able to try to describe it in retrospect, preferably by dealing with the process of its treatment.

During these Christmas holidays, I had hoped to have fourteen whole days set aside for writing; but there are long interruptions, errands, trips to the city. This means I have to take a new running start every morning. Furthermore, at this very moment, someone is using an electric drill on the concrete walls of the floor above me. . . . Nevertheless I want to try to immerse myself a little deeper today. This is the fourth day, and only now do I take a look at the clue cards I had prepared a few weeks ago. Having mentioned the noise, I pick up a noise clue: "Sneezing". That refers to the sneezing of the analyst, which might be described as a minor freak of nature. So I start out with the actual, while hesitating for a moment: am I violating discretion? But then I am not talking about a perversion or anything shameful: there is no harm in sneezing. My analyst suffers from periodical fits of it, and they always consist of three sneezes in a row. There is a sense of inevitability about it, as he himself claims, something trans- or metaphysical, and he never gave me permission to analyze it. On this point, he always fell back on physiology pure and simple, perhaps in order to prevent a reversal of roles. When the sneezing began, analysis was interrupted for a while, until the process had run its course. There was no absolute reason for this to be so. However, this is where my own reaction to his sneezing begins. As you may remember, the unknown person behind me underwent considerable fluctuations in fantasized dimensions of his size, depending on my interior state, sometimes achieving the magnitude of a true Moloch. The sneezing occurred without preparation and interrupted everything like a force of nature. It flung me into the ditch, as it were, I scurried for cover—not to mention the insult that the interruption was. At first I did not know the triple rhythm and tended to re-emerge from the ditch too soon, to rearrange my psychic limbs, carelessly, without cover. Then came the second explosion which threw me even farther out into the open. This time I took greater care while crawling back to the epicenter, flattening out at the first warning sound, however quiet, and thus survived the final blast relatively well. Then there was silence for a while. Then began the great blowing of the nose, the clean-up operation, a restless shifting about in the armchair, and even merry trumpeting sounds through the now-liberated nasal channel. After a further period of no activity on either side he said: "What is happening?" I drew a breath and replied: "Herr Doktor, that was like a natural phenomenon." I notice that I took refuge in irony from the very beginning, in regard to this episode; why, I do not know. For the benefit of the layman, I have to reiterate that the patient is cut off from the analyst except for words and sounds, and as a result of that, his acoustic perceptions gradually become sharper, almost like a blind person's, because of the great importance attached to the invisible person. When you feel quite small yet aware that the great one behind you is gripped by veritable spasms, and when you also perceive that instead of his otherwise gentle and comprehensible voice, these uncontrollable sounds are escaping from his mouth, the situation starts veering either in the direction of dinosaur zoology or of the cosmic. The cosmic interpretation was easy to arrive at because of the incredible noise, as was a religious interpretation because of the ritualistic triplicity. Whenever, for some unfathomable reason, one of these triads was not completed, I would express my dissatisfaction a little while later by remarking that the Holy Ghost had not yet given his opinion on the situation.

I am still not entirely contented with the description of my experience, so I'll start over, once again: Think about a two-year-old sitting on his father's lap, having just had a story read to him; now it is quiet, and then the gigantic figure against whom you are leaning starts shaking, and a thunder of giant noises strikes the ear. At first, the little fellow does not know what to think or do, seeing that the old man truly is of dinosaur size. The analyst's sneezing forcefully conveyed to me something about his physical presence, the piece of powerful paternal stature and the physicality that is subject to nature. That it impressed me to such an extent has to do with my actual father whose physicality, from the very first year of my life, was damaged and restricted by his illness, so that there was not much physical contact nor much cordial give-and-take with this dinosaur. Yet he, too, was able to sneeze like a primordial beast. In my regression, my father's body first seemed perennially alien, somewhat threatening or despicable. During a long analysis I then experienced the most varied stages of regression, among others, in regard to infant body contact and fantasies about the parents' bodies. There is more to be said about this later on. Here it was more a question of explaining in what way the sneezing first pulled me back into perceptions connected to shivering, fear, reverence, sometimes even malicious laughter. During the bad days of vulnerability the sneezing naturally acquired yet another meaning: he is sneezing out of boredom; he just wants to annoy me; that idiot's mind is on totally different matters—or: why is he sneezing just at this moment? is he punishing me? for the love of God, am I perhaps worthless after all and he doesn't like me anymore?

I just have to put myself back into that phase of vulnerability to remember a whole sequence of other noises emanating from him that impinged on my psychic life or disturbed my equilibrium. Sometimes I was able to hear his fingertips faintly drumming on the armrest: admittedly not often, but that only made it affect me harder. Once again I was gripped by the fear that he was bored, or that he was trying to suppress anger, or that he was elsewhere in his thoughts. The same applied when he was excercising his toes inside of a certain pair of shoes, making the leather creak quietly. The irritable child's most intense wish is to have father and mother pay exclusive and utmost attention to itself; given that, a creaking of shoes may seem like treason, enough to trigger anxiety or rage. When I talked to him about it, or rather, confessed my feelings with halting difficulty, he provided a beautiful image, obviously out of his own experience as a paterfamilias. "Do you know," he said, "sometimes when you are holding a child on your arm and another adult appears and you start talking to him and forget the child for a moment, it happens that the child grabs you by the ears and tries to turn your head around by force, to get your face to point at where he is sitting, and says: 'Hey, you, you should look at *me*, not at other people!' "

That was, indeed, my experience with him. Writing the words "experience as a paterfamilias" has made me wince under the onslaught of associations: for a moment, all the fits of jealousy against his children became evident again. I regarded his children as favorites of fate—they were princes and princesses, to be sure. However, I would like to postpone the large subject of jealousy for a while: for a little longer, I want to go on pretending that no other people have any part of him, are closer to and tighter with him than I am: that, I cannot endure yet.

Another memory surfaces, although it is of a later date. Once I noticed that he groaned, several times, during the session, as if something were hurting him considerably. Finally I asked him about it. He started in surprise, apologized, and told me that he was worrying about one of his children who was hospitalized, but that he had not noticed himself sighing. But at that time I was already able to ameliorate the jealousy by means of empathy, and thus the episode is remembered as a part of my discovery of him as a human being. I was going to say: as an extra-analytical moment. As if there were such a thing! It was, of course, a completely analytical one, even considering that a child's psychic maturation encompasses the realization of parental feelings that one had not been aware of before. Well, now I am just talking around my own emotional upset. I believe that I loved him, even though his sighs had nothing to do with me.

Not at that moment, but during others experienced similarly, just a few, the following happened to me: we had achieved a particular inner proximity, and that on a level where feelings still desire to be transformed into action, directly. I lay on the couch, every part of me striving physically toward him. This is the only way I can express it, because the condition can be clearly distinguished from the impulse to move my legs and arms so as to embrace him. This wanting to touch him affected the entire body, better still: all the muscles, regardless of whether they had anything to do with an actual locomotion toward him or not. And at the same time, all the corresponding flexors contracted to hold me back. Perhaps one way of looking at it would be to say that my entire musculature became libidinously excited and restrained itself with difficulty. In any case, this caused a state of pleasurable blockage resembling weightlessness, and while it was occurring I thought of the phrase "embracing with the brakes on". It was a kind of total enervation of the body, a floating state, the body consoling itself thus because it was not allowed to follow the soul to a more intense closeness.

There were, by the way, frequent situations in which I just lay there quietly, more or less depressive, and did not feel like talking. Often in those moments I tended to secretiveness, or rather, secretive joys. Apart from minor exceptions, it took me a long time to confess to these, way into the third year. My imagination started busying itself with his body. Let us begin with the more innocent things. It sometimes happened that the depression assumed a form that caused me to believe my face was skinless, bare, vulnerable. I could easily admit to that, as it was a sensation I had often had before: a feeling of emaciation, of vulnerability, and there really was no cure for the painful facial sensation except to press the face against a mother's cheeks. Yet I cannot remember ever having done exactly that. Nevertheless, the need to do so could grow very strong, and then I fantasized that the analyst put his hand on it, and later, growing bolder, that I hid my face in his; but there was no way I could say it. One of the early confessions occurred in connection with a memory out of my reading, from (I think) Hebbel's *Letters*. He writes about the death of a tame squirrel that used to come and hide in his armpit. That was my wish, too, when the need for shelter became strong. Milder versions of the wish involved sitting in his vest or coat pocket. As curiosity and orientation to the world grew stronger again, but the protective identity of little Thumbelina still seemed desirable, I wanted to sit in the outer breast pocket of his suit, sticking my head out and eyeballing the world from that safe vantage point. Once I dreamt that I had, Jonah-like, entered the inner space of his body and wandered about in it: the décor would have to be visualized as similar to the pictures by Richard Oelze whose work impressed me very much at that time, and the dream was borrowing from it.

The excursion to the interior was an exception. It appears that I had had quite a passable time in the womb—the sojourn there had been of sufficient duration and satiation, and thus I was not constantly fixated on a return. What's more, my mother was a trained and experienced pediatric nurse and I think she tried to make the world an inhabitable place for her firstborn, inasfar as that is possible outside of the maternal body—perhaps even *too* comfortable. I do not have my neurosis because I was born, in whatever technical fashion, but because the firstborn's expulsion from Paradise took place rather crudely—unmitigated by all manner of adverse circumstances. On the surface, all of this is mainly a question of transformation, of a clinging to aroused but unfulfilled infant wishes. As I have said, all confessions having to do with the wish for physical proximity were inordinately hard to make. No doubt this had to do with a degree of proscription of such things at home: both my grandfathers were, after all, Protestant clergymen of extremely rigorous moral character. Thus, my neurosis has truly been blessed by the Holy Ghost of Protestant puritanism, and to that it owes much of its persistence and weight.

I see that I have limited myself a little too much by this confession of secret fantasies that occurred when I was lying on the couch, not speaking. If I proceed now to another layer of the fantasies, there will be much to explain and to say in clarification that does not flow through the typewriter too easily. Therefore, this might be an opportune place to allow myself a breather and to report more on the analyst and his way of helping me in the preparation of confessions, and generally on his way of dealing with me in certain situations. Much of the time I was a taciturn patient, though not in a defiant, compulsively restrained, negating or camouflaging sense, except for certain of those fantasies. The silence had to do with my needs for autonomy, and also with my years if not decades of a habituation to solitude and its necessity to figure out things for oneself. Thus, my silence became more of a mutual communication problem in terms of what occurred in me while it lasted: should he try to break it, or remain equally silent, or interpret it, or just give me time? In the meantime I have learned from my own patients to how great an extent such silence confronts one with problems of both a technical and an emotional nature, even when one is sitting behind the couch.

Patiently he kept on trying to find out what silence might mean in my case. Later, when I had developed a better ability to split my ego, I was able to relate to him what was going on, not to leave him groping in the dark, waiting in vain, or straining himself unduly. There were things that I wanted to think and feel my way through alone, yet always in his presence. My silence often indicated an attempt to structure something. I remember one of his questions during a phase of silence: mildly, entirely without reproach, and, as it were, offering assistance in a way that I could refuse without offending him, he said, "Should I shut up, or can I say something?" I was moved by that, and moved to gratitude, and silently vowed to praise him for it one day. I had never experienced so much courtesy and tact in my life, that cautious query: I do not know if you can use my help at this moment, but I wanted to tell you, in any case, that I am here.

During the silence I started to inhabit an ever larger space within myself, figuratively speaking. Putting it another way, in his presence and with his assistance I was constructing my own inner space, and thus, while it was his space, too, or he was the architect of that ego space, he always knocked before entering. "May I say something?" he asked me, as soon as the silence had created a certain distance or uncertainty.

There were a few sessions during which I maintained total silence. When this happened, he made two or three tentative offers, probably in order to see whether I would not be able to talk after all, or whether I was in a bad mood, but I was not in a bad mood—although that was a reason, once—but not as a rule; then he just left me alone. Yet it could happen that I returned to him during the final quarter-hour, in order to relate my experiences and insights to him. I know that his patient silence entailed some sacrifices on his part, or that it did so at least some of the time, because he is a companionable person and thus cannot take being ignored for hours, not even in analysis, and certainly not after my having talked with him so extensively. No, I have to make this absolutely clear: he let me go and embark on my inward peregrinations, a little sorrowfully perhaps, regretting that there were so many ways I wanted to walk by myself. Later, I was able to reward him once in a while by acknowledging this or by reporting on my journey. When building a house there comes a point when one can go on by oneself, having worked long enough taking instructions. He has, indeed, slowly made me into the master builder of my own interior house: and that is not a 'slip', it is a startling clarification. It also reveals something about the bourgeois, if not grand-bourgeois atmosphere of this analysis. I was not always busy with this interior construction work: as I have said, I was often preoccupied by my secret fantasies about him and by the consolations I undertook to perform on him by means of various parts of the body; or else with stubborn resistance and the building of barricades. As he was exceptionally capable of empathizing with me and thus did not really have to rely on questions all that much, being able to scent and sense what was going on in my head, he would sometimes smile and ask me: "Having a nice quiet spell?" That would cause me to laugh out loud and to launch into a confession, total or partial, caught out as I had been. Or he would carefully, in various modulations, ask me: "What's happening?", so that I was left a great degree of freedom to answer or not to answer in any detail. Or he relied on that psychoanalytical *ur*-sound, the one that keeps thousands of psychoanalyses going in this world and still has not worn out, the famous and much-maligned "Mm". This "Mm" can be like a lifesaver thrown to a shipwrecked person, or it is like the first support of a bridge to be erected across a previously seemingly impassable river or canyon, or it is encouragement, indication of curiosity or compassion. However, when it is pronounced interrogatively or meditatively or skeptically, it can serve as a substitute for a whole raft of interpretations and indicate a detection. Or it is like a chewed-up bone that is thrown to you and that you want to fling back, barking furiously, with the accusation "I guess that's all you have to offer me today", or "Here one might starve to death without your even noticing, you clod", or "One more of those 'mms', and I'll strangle you!"

Far be it from me to deny that I often experienced his silence as something different from maximal courtesy and tact: that would be a misconception that I have to hasten to prevent. The analyst's silence can appear to be an act of punishment or archaic revenge, it can be like being left out in the cold, an indication of indifference, sarcasm, absence: or like the master's looking on as the servant laboriously tries to express some pitiful little insight. As a patient, you then pull out all stops in order to pierce through that wall of silence, with threats and supplications, flattery and attempts to make the other feel guilty, with overt or camouflaged accusations of canaillery, brutality, coldness, arrogance, stupidity, or of a blend of stupidity and perfidy. Does this help? Unfortunately, only rarely. One of the accusations that kept returning to my mind and emanating from my lips was: "Once again, and after having shelled out all that money, I have to make the analysis myself. I guess you don't have any further ideas today, once again, and it's still a long haul to retirement." As I now have patients myself, I am naturally subjected to a barrage of these accusations; to which I should add that I was, of course, unable to employ any feminine weaponry against *him*—whereas now, as if in punishment, I am being attacked with a much more extensive arsenal of urgency.

To procrastinate a little longer about my secret fantasies that often overwhelmed me on the couch, I want to mention an incident relating to the breaking through the so-called analytical situation and to the restraint in intercourse with the analyst outside his office. It is a ground rule that the analyst must not engage in any sociable activities whatsoever with his patients. He should remain anonymous, so that the patient, in the madness of transference, can freely attribute everything that arises in his psyche to *him*, unhampered by any actual knowledge of him. Yet all patients experience this as a gross imposition. From a certain moment on they become convinced, as I did and as many of my predecessors on the couch have done, that their happiness essentially *depends* upon their being allowed to fraternize with the analyst, in spite of all biblical and mythological and juridical injunctions against incest and related matters. I have already related his children's apotheosis, through envy, to the statue of princes and princesses. On the sly, my fantasies enlarged his house into a great manor or castle. I endowed his wife with truly divine qualities, and the metal of his automobile, when I happened to see it, became an object for furtive caresses. It was not just metal, it was meta-metal, and surely the front end did not contain just your usual, average, routine HPs, but something far more sophisticated. It is difficult to explain to the uninitiated the fantasies or wishes or actions arising out of regressed love mania—which can, of course, also be a hate mania, and normally is an ambivalent mania. This is exactly what the heretics and pagans and above all the educated scoffers see as the absurdity of the whole psychoanalytical undertaking: that the psyche, once again, starts acting like an infant.

I notice that irony tries to carry me away once again: which means that I am getting a little scared of the emotions I am uncovering. I was about to tell how transfiguration, for good or bad, started taking place, similar to the transfiguration of parents in young children. Well, just try to explain to those little children that their education will proceed much better if they get to see their beloved parents only for fifty minutes a day—any real 'seeing' occurring mostly only for a couple of seconds, before you keel over at the beginning and before you stagger out at the end. The infants would find this incomprehensible, and they would flatten their noses against the locked doors and try to peek through the tiniest cracks. They would collect rumors, interrogate third parties with varying degrees of finesse, or start conversations in order to direct them so that they will eventually come around to the parents. I, too, did all these things, in order to pick up a few grains of reality. Once I even perceived the great chance and opening that would permit me to get close to him. By combining my powers of sophistication with those of crude cunning, I managed to sit next to him at the drinking table at a conference, while still in therapy, with a glass of wine in my hand, just like a colleague among colleagues, a contemporary among his contemporaries. But that binge was followed by a hangover. The therapy really went into a spin, and the ironic camaraderie with which I attacked my idealization, my admiration, in short, the process of transference, proved to be useless; all it had created was inner chaos, cracks in the transference. Reality does not always correspond with the magic of idealization: this is not to say that my encounter with him was a fiasco, but simply that he then became a human being with his own demands, weaknesses, and wishes. The open space provided for the analytical patient's unfolding suddenly disappears, embarrassment takes over, there is an urgent desire to "grab the opportunity", but what opportunity *is* there? The real opportunity is provided by the analyst's precise management of the transference, by his abstinence, my abstinence, by the gradual unfolding of the transference neurosis.

Thus, it is futile to imagine that it could be possible to establish a genuine relationship out of the midst of transference. Even while pretending to be sensible, one is spinning wildly all over the place. While one is engaged in acquiring the tools of the trade, one is inevitably tempted to create situations with the future older colleagues, impatiently, ahead of time, which are mere sacrifices on the altar of infantile attraction, while masquerading as innocent, professionally or educationally necessary approaches. That does not preclude one's discovery of, perhaps, even a great many aspects of the analyst that can make friendship with him into a truly desirable goal. In disbelief and unable to resist my own impulses, I attempted a few more of these approaches, although less blatantly, getting burnt time and again, until I realized, at last, that I had to protect the principle of abstinence myself. Thereafter I have done much to keep the analytical situation as pure as possible, free from any additives of quotidian intercourse; and that probably was my last chance.

I notice that the preceding passage has become imbued with pedagogical zeal. This may be due to a sense that the inner struggle for abstinence has not yet ceased entirely, and possibly to the fact that I myself now get to experience my patients' urges to get closer to me: thus I can compare the sacrifices they have to make, or that I have to demand from them, with my own. Every so often one hears about all that happens in neighboring analytical counties as soon as there is a slacking-off from the principle of abstinence. At first, it may sound fascinating, but later the shrug becomes the dominant reaction. In any case, I would have been de-railed for sure, had a lack of discipline prevailed on both sides.

I am drawing closer to the fantasies. My experience of writing parallels the analysis itself. I am asking for extensions and granting them to myself. This was, indeed, often the case: certain motifs heralded themselves by means of notions, situations, dreams, and then submerged again, or rather, *were submerged*. The exact term for that being: they were repressed again. Particularly opportune times for the appearance of new motifs or the making of confessions were the final days before a break in the analysis. I was really good at that: at flashing some emotions, once, and then taking a powder. He was quite relentless in pointing this out to me, with varying degrees of success. The unconscious, too, is cunning, or at least cautious—to be exact, this applies to those unconscious parts of the ego whose task it is to do guard duty on the walls of defensiveness.

A brief digression may be permitted, as it fits well with the subject of the urge to proximity, whether inside or outside of the analysis. For example, the need to shake hands with him as soon as I set eyes on him could at times become uncommonly urgent. At such moments the mere fact that he was making a telephone call, waving a greeting, and mainly and quite rightly paying attention to the intruder at the other end of the line, was enough to throw me off balance.

At first, there were unsuccessful handshakes, as when, for instance, I only managed to get hold of two of his fingers, or to stick one of my own between our palms in a curious fashion. That could be embarrassing until it had been talked about—trivia such as that mainly provided cause for mutual amusement, on the solid ground of our relationship. There was also the problem of the duration of the handshake: such complicated, strenuous processes while solving the conflict, only lasting fractions of seconds, as to who lets go first. At times phobic or counter-phobic or otherwise knotted up, and in any case determined not to betray myself, I took his hand as if it had been a hot iron that might burn, or a sticky something that one might be caught on for the rest of one's life.

The brief act of getting up off the couch can become a torture if one is ashamed of one's body or thinks one is naked or that a bent knee betrays the insolent desire for a fiery embrace. One day I saw him disappear into the toilet, before the beginning of our session; according to my cautious calculations he spent sufficient time in there to void himself thoroughly. Then he returned, and with a certain embarrassment, yet with a feeling of gladness, I extended my hand to him. What did he do? He went over to the handbasin and washed his hands, most meticulously. I was hurt. I was not yet able to discuss the emotional implications during that session, but there were great rumblings inside me, because the frustration caused by the hand stretched out in vain had been considerable. In the next session, I took a running start and said among other things: "Herr Doktor, I think I really would not mind your having a couple of little lumps of shit sticking to your palm, as long as I don't have to wait so long to shake your hand."

There is no help for it, the fantasies are becoming more urgent, and I believe I have to show my true colors now. There is no need for me to begin with the higher or rather deeper analytical mathematics. Simple arithmetic will do: The analyst's head is possessed of a chin which one can fondly scratch, either when the dinosaur is lying down and sleeping, or when one is sitting on his arm or lap. He has a mouth that can snap shut, and yet one would like to stick one's finger into it. That is quite wonderfully terrifying-exciting, even only in fantasies. There is the nose in which one can search for the origin of things by poking until one gets flung out by its sneezing. And then, the ears, to be grabbed or to be used to turn the head in the desired direction. As is obvious, I am, as it were, stuck to the head, perhaps because I used to regard it as an innocent part of the body, hoping that the origin of things would be found there. But no matter how painful it is, even *my* terrestrial origins lie elsewhere, not in the head of Zeus, and soon the head will prove insufficient for my research. For a while I still clung to a story from Indian mythology in which the divine child is created by a white elephant's sticking his trunk into the goddess's ear. In accordance with my resistances, progress slowed down on my way down the body. At first, I was struck by his shoulders; I allowed myself to explore them with my hands, the juncture of neck and shoulder, the width of the shoulders, including biceps and triceps. It was a magnificent fellow I was sculpting there. "Taking the measure" is what I called it, meaning thereby: penetrating the secret of the male body which I had never approached in the case of Laios, out of awe for his illness. After the shoulders, there was the first break in tactile exploration. In my fantasies I ran around the room as a little boy who runs away from the old man and then runs back again. That was, in fact, what I was actually doing at the time—at least it would be possible to interpret my urge to travel and be an itinerant preacher: running away and coming back, every week two lectures in faraway locations, and on top of that, trips to weekend conferences, until exhaustion enforced abstinence on me even in this matter. A beautiful fantasy: to stand between the analytical father's knees, looking at the world, elbows leaning on his knees, such securely anchored to the old man. Or to perform gymnastic exercises between his knees, until one day my foot, swinging backwards, as if accidentally yet with great accuracy struck his testicles. In my fantasy, he then groaned a little. I pretended surprise but innocence was over. *En passant:* I had an almost insurmountable resistance to assume the gymnastic posture between his knees with my face at times turned toward his body. There simply was that thing in his pants that filled me with fearsome respect as well as immense curiosity. I had to take great pains to dare, in my fantasies, to run my fingertips exploratorily over his balls and to admit that I was doing so, while still keeping my shy distance from the patriarchal rod.

In general, this phase of approach was preceded by a long period of depreciation, even negation, of his masculinity. I literally clung to the maternal transference which in the meantime had become relatively harmless. Whenever he cautiously mentioned indications of paternal transference, I insisted on sardonically calling him "Mommy" or doubting that he was at his (a man's best) age still capable of an erection—this whenever the situation was more ambiguous, and it was harder to negate his gender. The tendency to depreciate the male in him was massive, of long duration, and one of the explanations we found for it later was that behind a rather weak image of Laios, another, archaic, terrifying and very potent one had been arrested: it was one I was truly afraid of, it was the Moloch who devours his children while continuously siring new ones.

I won't, at this stage, succeed in rendering the entire process of hesitation, of shrinking back from his physicality. Instead, I am reminded of the later period's conciliatory images, and of one before all others. I have climbed up his body as if it were a great tree, and now I am sitting, resting, looking out upon the world, at the root juncture of the first big erect branch growing out of the paternal oak. Above me, like a protective canopy, the paternal acorn. For a while this was a peaceful image. Then I noticed that my dangling heels were banging against his testicles, and this, naturally, was cause for instant fears of punishment and revenge. I realize that all this might sound a little impertinent, especially if I weren't capable of making clear the torture and duration of shame connected with it during the analysis. A genuine neurotic blindness had to be remedied before the fantasies showed themselves at all, and a disturbance of speech, before I was able to speak about them, and an impediment to writing, before I was, now am, able to write about them. Numerous supportive interpretations to placate the noisy superego were required before I became more courageous. The supportive element related primarily to the fact that I, since I was totally underdeveloped in physical encounter with the masculine, immediately connected every emerging fantasy with a fear of manifest homosexuality and thus became really frightened. This is where the second level of paranoid reaction opens up. Not only did I believe that he wanted to seduce me, I also feared that he wanted to turn me into a homosexual, or that, at least, he was thoughtlessly permitting this to happen. Or I was plunged into the fear that I was really homosexual and just had not wanted to believe it, and saw my experiences and relationships with women wiped off the slate, as mere pseudo-heterosexual, defensive theatricals. . . . I have to shelve the subject once again for a while: it is getting to be hard going. Thus, again, a couple of episodes that do not consume so much energy against resistance, or where the resistance has really become a thing of the past. I wanted to purchase a new automobile, the first new one after a series of second hand VWs and a little plastic Lloyd, and worried about the problem of how much to spend and how to compromise between practical considerations, comfort, and self-image. It took me three weeks to work my way through the question, and we discovered all kinds of things in regard to problems of potency, exhibitionism, speed, sibling rivalry, need for camouflage and guilt feelings. We can skip all of them; they are, as it were, self-explanatory. The supreme moment came when the final result of all these tortuous considerations was unveiled. One Monday morning, as the analyst arrived in his car, I suddenly saw it all: the make and color of my new vehicle were the same as his, only the model was a little smaller. I was totally incapable of judging whether I even liked that color—it could be justified with a great number of rationalizations—but the unconscious certainly had deemed it the most beautiful, although I really did not have any primary and spontaneous relationship with "desert brown".

In terms of externals, this probably was the highest point of identification. There were certain inhibitors, even barriers to identification, though hardly any in the realm of analysis as craft: there I really found almost no reasons not to admire and to imitate him. But a strange twilight resulted in processes like the following. He would lightly comment on the fact that I was wearing new shoes or a new pair of pants. It goes without saying that those were cautious invitations: well, young fellow, what does clothing mean to you, does anything come to mind in regard to the new shoes? How does it feel to live in those new trousers? When exhibitionism, as a partial urge, has not been submerged entirely, but awaits (which would certainly fit with the churchy origins of my repression) its resurrection in the basement or up in the attic, only barely restrained by its wrappings in the old chest, then any new clothing certainly involves resistance and counter-cathexis, to use those bits of professional jargon: in other words, it is safe to assume that a ghostly battle begins backstage, between superego, shame, training and the liberated urges to show. Well-aimed interpretations dealt, e.g., with the billowing commodiousness of the trousers I would buy and in which nothing could be seen of my actual physicality, quite contrary to the increasingly urgent edicts of male fashion at the time. It is quite possible, even probable, that the width of those pants was quite openly protective against the fears of seduction that I did not know how to deal with at that time. Thus, it was possible for clothing to be expression or obfuscation of sexuality on one hand, and on the other—and this is what I meant by the term 'twilight'—there was the great temptation to let him lavish narcissistic care on me, like a girl, and thus, finally, to be caressed by his eyes and compliments and admiring hands.

That wish was reversible, as well. When I found out that he played the piano, I immediately dreamt that I was playing duets with him, and told him about it in all innocence. But it was not innocent play: on closer scrutiny, the keyboard turned out to be the keyboard of his body which was enticing me.

Time and again there were the fantasies of 'measuring': a passion for research had erupted in my psyche. I felt the need to visualize his body exactly, to recreate its topography in my mind, and also to wrestle with him, to press against his chest, pitting my strength against his—to give my own body form and stature through the resistance of his body. All this frightened me a great deal. I squirmed in the throes of resistance and unwillingness to permit it. It is obvious that I was, at least in my imagination, infatuated with him in a fairly clear-cut homosexual fashion, although I never fantasized or dreamed about orgiastic sexual scenes with him, in the traditional sense of our giving each other mutual libidinous satisfaction. Some interpretations genuinely alleviated this fear, and so did a bit of theory that he incorporated in them: e.g., on the connection between infantile homosexuality and masculine identification with the father. Not all of it was, by any means, manifest homosexuality in the commonly understood sense, and only rarely was I gripped by an inclination to look for such contacts in real life. It was rather a kind of infantile sex research, a belated passion for the inaccessible body of Laios, and during that time, memories surfaced of scenes where I had been watching, enviously, healthy fathers at play with their children: watching them climb up on them, fighting with them, hug them and race with them. Illness had made Laios even more reticent in physical contact than he had probably been anyway, and now that entire wish, obviously repressed with great difficulty, for paternal physicality broke through again. "Taking the measure" became a key phrase, not least because it gradually became apparent that I did not possess an entirely stable, interior and unconscious feeling for my body. For a number of years at school I had engaged in sports almost addictively, going beyond the point of enjoyment, often to the edge of exhaustion. Very slowly it became apparent how this connected with the struggle against shame and with the search for an acceptable feeling for my body—which nevertheless, despite all the athletic activity, was liable to collapse rapidly.

I felt myself to be misshapen, not human in form. One curious aspect of the matter: there is a differentiated, unconscious body scheme in regard to women and to men. Physically reliable proprioception in regard to the women was achieved independently after much searching, and it probably connected back to the good care taken of me as an infant and young child. But the uncertainty within this male body towards other males erupted quite massively, nourishing the equally addictive practice of "measuring up against": Who am I in my body, what does it look like, how does it feel in relation to another male body?

The unreliability of my body feeling had practically prevented me from taking part in any fights. I can remember only two occasions. On these, the bitter truth became apparent, emerging from the cover of the libidinous possibilities of such showdowns, and it was what enabled me to fight at all: that the body seemed to be useable as a weapon only in situations of absolute emergency. For a long time I tortured myself with the suspicion that my abstinence from fighting was cowardice. The resistance against homosexual enticements became more panic-stricken against that background, as several needs and instincts converged into it. It also cut me off from any corrective experiences. While in college, I once joined a judo club, but abandoned the endeavor after a short while, because I found it impossible to use my body as a weapon with the required determination. I was unable to throw someone on the floor after holding him in my arms, or over my shoulder, and I felt hurt and sad whenever I became aware that the other's embracing hold on me was only aimed at hurling me down onto the mat.

My analyst had a remarkable understanding of this desire to take the measure. For a while, I experienced it as something not unlike wrestling with the Lord's angel: "I will not let go until you bless me": with a part of my identity, and with my ability to inhabit my own body. As soon as my perception of these early developments in my physical existence became more acute, it also became clearer why my relationships with women had not resulted in a solid psychic body surface: women *allow* themselves to be grabbed and formed and brought into a transitory stance, they rarely engage in shaping, themselves, in that architectural sense of a defining drawing-of-contours of the body. They caress it, but they do not provide it with contours. They slide over the interior deformations and lacunae of shape, without filling them in.

The question arises whether any of this imaginative experience has any meaning or effect: and while I am asking myself that question, I become uncertain. Why do I now have the feeling that I have, after all, made myself more at home in my body —that the experiences of deformation and alienation, even terror, have diminished in intensity? There probably is some degree of innervation going on during those fantasies, a kind of experimental activity in the musculature; this became quite evident in the scene with the "embraces with the brakes on".

As another aspect of this disturbance of my body perception, I often did not experience my penis as a part of my body: I always thought of the word "exterritorial" in regard to it. The pubic area—*Schamgegend* in German—was indeed a shameful zone, always suspect of possible stench, that of urine. According to my inner experience, the prick was a ridiculous and despicable object, nothing to be proud of but a flaw, rather embarrassing to look at, yet simultaneously and nevertheless the instrument and prime location of lust: and that creates a mighty ambivalence. And the curious thing is that even its appropriate and enjoyable use, alone or with a partner, was not capable of entirely healing or minimizing that exterritoriality and sense of its not belonging to the body, not quite. There always remained a residue of guilt (or, "the shit stuck to the stick", as the German saying goes). While I was going over all that in the analysis, suffering great pangs of shame, I remembered an illuminating scene that no doubt heralded the cure, over a decade ago. A female friend was lying beside me. We had been making love by an open window with the sun streaming in, an Arcadian picture. We were drinking red wine. As if to test it, she took the now inert little fellow into her hand, raised her wine glass above it and baptized it, its commendable existence, its legitimate and flawless being. At that moment, a great deal of grim and puritanical self-scorn left it, quite demonstrably, or at least became more endurable, giving me an inkling of freedom and legitimate belonging, one that the analysis could relate to later.

At this point, I am sure, it is time once again for a bit of self-justification. I can feel how many of you will decide not to stay with me any longer, turning away, repulsed, or enraged and offended, or invoking the necessity to protect the young. Don't I have anything more important, more elevating, more relevant to the family and the people to say than all this inflated talk about the so-called exterritoriality of a penis? I have to admit that they are right. It is possible to live with an exterritorial penis, to sire children with it, even to provide and to experience enjoyment with it, without even becoming aware of its condition. But this is what I am about: I am trying to find out of what the unhappiness of my neurosis consisted, where it came from and how it was ameliorated. My disturbed body feeling, including that of the alter ego, caused me to experience alienation, frequently paralysis, and this had a very negative effect on my basic inability to form satisfying human relationships. It is possible to reconcile oneself to difficulties in contact with others, even when these become painful. They are the rule rather than the exception. I was not able to live with them, probably because I had an unconscious memory from early infancy that told me things had not always been this way, and that I should not, therefore, resign myself to the present state. Choosing psychoanalysis, I chose, with negative results at first, a form of therapy that attacks such matters with the well-known Freudian vigor: not content with half-measures, it wants to pursue the disturbances back to their origins. As I have chosen this path and am now—although I still have not reached the end—looking back on the long distance covered with gratitude, I want to continue on it, and to describe it, even when confronted, with increasing frequency, with the faces of acquaintances who regard this as incomprehensible and even deplorable for a great variety of reasons. Yet I am to some degree reassured by my own conviction that all of it is merely a case of the quite averagely human, in an individual manifestation.

It is possible that the continued analytical work, five hours a week, has caused at least temporarily a state of over-cathexis in regard to psychic events—which is not at all unusual—and it may be that in the wake of the "exterritoriality" of so many things in my neurosis, there has also been an over-emphasis on physical events, as their significances are gradually changed by the analysis. Thus I find it difficult to regard the peculiar form of exhibitionism I now need to indulge in in order to write as a deplorable and constant trait. I try to explain it to myself by the realization that the "success" of this fourth attempt at analysis strikes me as so unaccustomed and so linked to an alert sense of contrasts and nuances that experiencing and describing no longer occur as far apart as they did on the first try. I can remember certain sessions during which caution obviously had me keep emotional volume down very low, and also made me think enviously of those who are able to engage their own neurotic disease analytically at the very first attempt. They just fall into analysis, as it were, hardly knowing later what it was that happened to them. Thus, I assume that I am enthusiastic about my analyst who was finally able to create a useful analysis with me while I was watching him, skeptically, comparatively, then again with amazement and gratitude, and equally enthusiastic about myself, having slowly shed my inability to permit anyone to help me. All this is justification, even to myself, when I go into great detail about the re-structuring of my inner organs.

I have experienced the Freudian "operation" without the customary narcosis of the observing consciousness and without a narcosis of the speech center, and would find it hard to bury this rare experience in silence, especially since the experience itself found its medium *in language* for long stretches of the way. I shall be accused of exhibitionism, and I admit that I was afraid, tonight, that this undertaking was a false trail, and had to engage in verbal self-encouragement. If I am to persist, things will come to light that will take me into far more intimate realms. For example, as every initiate will have asked himself, what about masturbation? Customarily, it is a particularly significant mode of consolation for depressives. I have had to console myself a lot that way, even at times when there was no visible need for it. It is often a final weapon in the battle against an extreme feeling of impoverishment, and considering the accompanying fantasies, it does create at least fictitious contacts. It is, furthermore, a way of dealing with the fears of castration, to be exact: with the fear that one has already been castrated. In the course of normal development, it—among other things—advances the striving toward relationships. Yet it also has to do with the unfolding of autonomy. As I was heavily dependent on many unconscious ties to my parents and relations, masturbation frequently had yet another value, connected with stubborn rebelliousness: I don't need any of you, I am sufficient unto myself. Admittedly, there is a tragic element in such exclusive reliance on masturbation, as it then becomes an attempt to pull oneself out of the swamp of loneliness and feelings of worthlessness by one's own hair or tail. It is a lonely triumph, shared with no one, and it does not, in reality, effect any change in that self-rejection: thus, it never brings about any progress, but is merely a compensation for stagnation.

When there are no actual partners, and the devaluation of the body has reached a high degree, desperate attempts are made to find a solution. One of these is true exhibitionism: there, if one cannot make mother's eyes shine any more, one can at least make them widen in terror. Looking for a substitute for that 'shine', I arrived in front of mirrors, in desperate self-admiration: "Well then, take a look, any of you who think this isn't a man!" Perversions do not nourish but end in hangovers. My dependency on mirrors certainly was a form of perversion. That, merely as a preliminary to the description of a stretch of therapeutic process: one, fairly soon after the beginning of analysis, I told my analyst in a mood of genuine surprise that I had masturbated the day before, after coming home from the session, entirely free of guilt feelings! The analyst was not surprised. In a calm voice and perhaps even with a trace of therapeutic satisfaction, he explained that he assumed he had been, in some sense, present at that feast. This was indeed true, although it is hard to express in concrete terms. Let us say that he was present in that space, approving, accepting, protecting, and thus the joy was no longer solitary but the expression of a strong relationship. Although this was only a beginning, it still was *the* beginning of the end of the banishment of sexual pleasure to illegal, lonely, peripheral zones of experience. The body's instinctive wishes were once again directed toward a beloved human being. His interpretations proved an immense relief to me. Just imagine: here one has tortured oneself for years, especially during one's Christian adolescence, with feelings ranging from failure to damnation, and now one is told by another one who is the object of love and admiration and who has, for the time being, taken over a portion of that sick conscience: "I am glad that you are building these bridges to me."

That was the beginning of a passion for him, and as my fears of homosexuality did not allow me to experience it openly and without inhibitions, it proceeded through many circuitous channels, smoldering, opening out into many other areas.

Thus, a few months later, I experienced the following: I had been invited to participate in a public symposium in a far distant city. It was a painful occasion, I was in a bad mood, did not really get going, finally did not want to talk to anybody any longer. I had been put up in a luxurious hotel room, distinguished by an enormous mirror, almost wall-sized and indirectly lit. When I came back from the gabfest, depressed and worn out, I got out of my clothes in record time. The adjustable, direct and indirect lighting—there were several moveable lamps at my disposal—became a medium I manipulated like the Mannerist painters used their light sources. For at least an hour I busied myself with optical body art, performing calisthenics, exhibiting myself, going into all kinds of contortions. It was like a narcissistic high, tinged, after ejaculation, with shame and bitterness, yet not to such a degree that everything would have collapsed again. As it was an extraordinarily strong experience, it did, of course, come up in my analysis. I have rarely suffered such pangs of shame as during that session. The labor of confession made me sweat, and after I had managed to relate the experience, with much hemming and hawing, I was exhausted and felt like running away. But what happened was strange and unexpected. He said: "I have a feeling that we have, here, set foot on hallowed soil—together." For a moment I almost forgot to breathe. I was inwardly torn: on one hand, endlessly grateful, on the other, racked by critical spasms. The words seemed to me far too large, too bombastic, too religious. I was not really able to shift gears, from such Christian vocabulary to actual life events. But that interior critic was soon silenced. I thought: don't judge him by the words, but by your feelings. And, after a while, I said: "I was just overcome. Here I returned, full of shame, and you provided a festive reception." That understanding of a narcissistic ecstasy came to play a sustaining part, as a memory and even as one of the cornerstones of our relationship. The reception made a huge chunk of fear vanish forever, the fear of the extent of my suppressed physical narcissism. It had broken through in an uncontrollable, excessive way, but that, exactly, diminished its impact. To express the event in an image: each fiber of my body that I had admired, all alone by myself, in the mirror and its changing light, wound itself around the analyst, during the confession and thereafter. I was rid of the fear that this long pent-up physical narcissism might be so powerful that it would, as it were, devour my ability to engage in close relationships with other people. At the same time, I believe that this kind of narcissism must be far more common than we think, although hidden by repression and always acted out only by proxy, by the professionals of fashion, of the stage or of the television screen.

There were hard battles around the aforementioned smoldering passion for the analyst, ranging from violent accusations directed at him to the feeling that I was or was no longer able to develop the necessary form of love-in-transference. Their starting point, time and again, lay in my fears of homosexuality which for a long time had resulted in fantasies about being seduced by him. There were a few incidents, apparently minuscule yet of great consequence, that kept me trapped in these seduction fears, or that I allowed to do so. To clarify that, I have to digress a little. I do realize, now, that it can be technically difficult for an analyst to deal with a subject, or to advance it cautiously, the investigation of which is evidently crucial for the progress of the analysis, and which is hedged around with such massive resistances. Thus, the analyst will drop the occasional hint, feeling his way to see if it is time to take the next little step. As I was hypersensitive in that particular context, even such cautious attempts were transformed into evidence of the seduction plan. There was another factor coming into play: my defiance. I felt trapped. I sensed that the feelings and fantasies were becoming clearer. I knew that I had to make my way through them. I assumed that that was what he was waiting for, and thus I maneuvered myself into a situation I experienced as follows: There he sits, back there, knowing he can wait, knowing I'll give in. It's just like some strategy to exhaust me, a race in which the hedgehog always makes it to the goal line before the hare. He became a watcher in the shadows, coolly and confidently watching the net tighten around his prey. And now my pride entered the unholy alliance: He wants to bring you to your knees, and then you are at his mercy. He can do anything he wants with you, wrap you round his little finger. I accused him of being a homosexual, himself, or that he had found a just about permissible form of sublimation in analyzing young men like myself and making them erotically dependent. I called him a Pied Piper who cast spells on everybody in order to ruin them. Nevertheless, occasional fantasies and events managed to break through my barriers of projection and negation. Once, when I hesitantly complimented him on a blue pinstripe suit he was wearing, I noticed, full of rage and shame, that I was feeling an itch in my pubic region. I had to muster all my strength in order not to scratch myself. But I did not want to give him any further clues: my pursuer was breathing down my neck already. The itch grew worse and worse, until I could not stand it anymore and told him I felt a thousand crab lice were working on the follicles of my pubic hair. And he said: "Oh, that's an interesting area." Cool triumph is what I heard in that utterance. Thus I felt shot down and did not broach the subject for a few weeks, until my paranoia received further nourishment from another episode. During the initial months I used to cross my legs while lying on the couch. Even after I found it possible to lie there without crossing them, I would hurry to re-cross them as soon as a subject made me feel uneasy. But a small interpretation had already attached itself to my prick. I consolidated into a certainty the notion that he would like nothing better than to slowly make me fixate on my pubic region so that he could then busy himself with my great tail. I purchased the wide pair of trousers mentioned before which presented nothing but a big fold even when I had my legs spread apart, and from then on, I made it a permanent habit to spread them thus, as if to set a trap of my own for him: If he grabs me now, I've caught him in the act, the despoiler of young boys!

There were times when I must have submitted him to genuine tortures by means of such projections, even though he was able to recognize the degree of my fear in them. As it seemed, after a few months, that the war around the pubic area was dying down and that it would be possible to discuss my sensations analytically, once again, I made yet another border incident into the occasion for extensive camouflage. I told him that I had masturbated in the toilet of a train while on a trip to give a lecture, exactly during the time of the analytical session that I was playing hooky from, to relieve a feeling of unease. Once again there was much shame involved, but I was also trying to connect the experience with the moving train, its rocking motion, the protected feeling of being a passenger that I occasionally experience while traveling on trains, quite philobatically: the well-being upon departure. He asked me: "Could you describe *how* you masturbated, what I mean is, the technique you used?" I experienced that as a brutal attack. There always are such momentary disruptions of empathy—if this was one at all—and if they result in a feeling of hurt, they can be talked about. This incident, however, ended in a retreat without discussion, I simply said "No" and was silent and later switched onto another subject, thinking: Whatever you do, don't show the sonofabitch your penis, he'll grab it without mercy. Many months later I bought the incident up again and tried to explain my frightened withdrawal and the impression I had received of his lack of empathy. He said: "I vaguely remember, I think I had just been reading an article about the connection between masturbatory practices and certain inner conflicts, and thus it possibly was a purely investigative question; I can well understand how you felt. I believe that I was paying too much attention to *my own* interests." That loosened the cramp, and gradually it became easier to discuss such matters successfully.

During the summer vacation following that phase, I had my first genuine homosexual experience, although it was—as in my fantasy—of limited sexual extent. Almost as a matter of course it happened that, far away from my domicile, after long conversations over red wine, I went to bed with a friend. *I* was the seducer, with a nonchalance that surprised myself. There was no fear, there were no threats uttered by my conscience, and I was so certain of my wooing that I was able to envelop him in that certainty. It was a shy, mutual exploration by touch, carefully avoiding the pubic region—more than carefully, almost reverently. It was not a question of carnal desire, I even shrank back when I felt his rod jutting out from his body like a length of iron. It was that marveling taking measure that played such a great part in my fantasies about the analyst. I traced his form, and he traced mine: it was a question of the feeling of similarity or identity. The experience made me glad, and there was no subsequent dimming of the memory. I was proud to have crossed that frontier, as it were, experimentally. It was connected with a diminution of fear, and perhaps with an imperceptible diminution of the need to frantically keep my distance from other men's bodies. It became easier to distinguish between sexuality and libidinous, friendly approach.

At this point, it seems appropriate to say something about "acting out," so called. There is no doubt that there was a good deal of acting out in this experience, a degree of release for the suppressed and smoldering passion for my analyst. That does not devalue the experience: I gave the friend what was his due. Not that that would always be the case: I confess that I have engaged in coitus at times without really being with my partner in my inner self. During the time of that summer vacation I already felt my relationship with the analyst to be so solid that I was able to talk to him about it without feeling threatened by his interpretations, i.e., without having to be afraid that he would snatch the experience from me and spoil it by simply referring it to the region of transference, to acting out. This was not always the case. Much earlier in the analysis we had a severe falling out, lasting two weeks, and I thought I had come a cropper once again and was correspondingly dismayed. I had taken a girl friend on a skiing vacation and felt that I had opened up new spaces in my relationship with her. When I returned to the couch, I soon got the impression that all I was offering was slapped out of my hand. I did, no doubt, exaggerate his interpretations that pointed out to me that much of what I had experienced was tinged by the state of my transference to him; but those interpretations undermined my feeling of my own worth and the need to lead a relatively independent existence. I misunderstood it to be an either-or choice: "Psychically, you can live only with me, or with someone else"—and if it had been a question of that, I probably would have opted for him. Yet I was also fighting against the devaluation of my friend. I yelled at him: "I won't let you turn this girl into some cheap substitute for yourself during the break in analysis." A statement like that positively reeks of guilt feelings toward the partner, but they were guilt feelings in regard to a primitive superego, an either-or superego. It was a bitter episode and marked the high point of a long-heralded feeling that I have already mentioned: the feeling that the analysis temporarily puts one's life in a state of suspension during which it is impossible to say anything exact about the really valid feelings towards individual persons. No doubt some of my previously described persecution mania contributed to the wild protest: the Moloch is trying to swallow me whole, he does not permit me to have any life outside of my attraction to him. At this date I can no longer differentiate as to how much of this was sheer projection, or how much, better, how little actual cause there was for me to act as offended as I did. Considering the onslaught of the feelings of starved returning patients, it is conceivable that he did not strike the customary empathetic note immediately. Maybe he was a little impatient in analyzing the vacation experiences, and my insult threshold certainly was a low one. Looking back, I can say that the fight with him and with my sense of having been offended was worth it. When it was over, after a fortnight, our relationship was on a more even keel than ever. At the same time, I had won a space for my autonomy: not that the analysis was not allowed in there, but that I was able to endure being analyzed there without fear. Another thing: I had the curious feeling of having, as it were, fought for the "honor" of that girl friend. She was not a stopgap lover and extra-analytical pastime, even though the passions might have intermingled. She had not disappeared in the voracious craw of the Moloch Analysis, but had retained a form of her own.

During an even earlier phase of the analysis, the one that I have mentioned as the phase of sucking sexuality, I made it a habit to have intercourse with my girl friend (whenever I stayed the night with her) shortly before going to my analytical session, mostly at nine in the morning; I kept this up for several months. I wafted onto the couch off a roseate cloud, the first few times full of naive pride, unaware of the significance of my cocky cheerfulness, until nourished by cautious interpretations, guilt feelings and (later) insight materialized, and that during a session, if memory serves, which I opened insolently, blasphemously, and traitorously to myself, by quoting the first line of the Christmas carol "Vom Himmel hoch, da komm ich her" ("From Heaven on high, whence I come"). Again I have to say that the interpretations did not diminish or inhibit the boisterous *joie de vivre* of those breakfasts in bed enriched with sexual pleasure. The acting out was mostly directed to the timing of sexual activity, and, among other things, to the elimination of superfluous libido, which was, as I believed, driving me towards a homosexual catastrophe, before 'dangerous' sessions.

I would like to address myself briefly to the arrival of new siblings on the couch. Once in a while it so happened that another one had arrived, and then one had to pass a new face on the stairs or in the entrance hall. This caused inner turmoil, every time, although its intensity slowly decreased after the fifth or sixth new arrival. As most of them were males, I wove them into sidelines of my persecution mania, sarcastically chuckling to myself that my analyst was probably indulging in his murky paedophiliac practices under the respectable cover of the YMCA. Well, I had wanted to get away from the subterraneanly smoldering passion, but I notice how that gets progressively harder. Thus, it is time to relate a couple of incidents during which I was no longer able to negate that state I was in. As the embers started glowing brighter, I experienced difficulties in walking whenever I had to walk next to him, say down the hall: these seemed to start from my hips, and I was no longer able to control entirely the motions of my legs. After I had, frivolously, walked up four flights of stairs next to him on the way to his office for a couple of times, it seemed to me that the difference between that climbing of stairs with him and a regular instance of sexual intercourse with him was becoming negligible. Thereafter I decided to negotiate the stairs by myself like a good boy, letting him use the elevator by himself.

I have already hinted at certain barriers to identification that prevented me from giving in to the smoldering and its consequences in all inner realms. For one thing this was perhaps due to an inner, belatedly recognized chasm between my archaically violent, yet entirely unreal father image, the later image of the father weakened by illness, my dream image of manliness that was diffuse and nebulous, and my perception of the analyst.

As I have mentioned, I kept on calling him "Mommy" even at the age of over two years, when my intelligence would have been quite sufficient for the perception of sexual differences. One might say that I experienced him as a maternal man. Something was missing in the picture I had of him: the ability to have things one's way, the exercise of power, public recognition, perhaps even ruthlessness. He was not a man I was afraid of, at least not as during the maternal transference, but, again, this was only so because I kept on pushing those Moloch fantasies ahead of me for years. Which is to say: from his person as I perceived it, nothing primarily frightening was emanating, and thus it took a long time until the archaic transference tendencies found any room to operate in. Besides, I simply held him captive within the frame: good weak father. Yet I had had to fight Jocasta for my rights to express myself as a man, and thus had to repeat that battle in the transference against the analyst whom I experienced as female for a long time, but not to such a degree against him as the father. Only where he really was an authority, in psychoanalytical matters, there was subterranean rivalry which was soon to change into grateful identification. There he was simply the teacher of the craft whom I trusted.

An important factor, repeatedly, in the course of the analysis, was my inability to regard him as my model in certain areas, which caused me to unconsciously experience him as insufficient. Yet I was late in discovering these connections, with his help. For a long time he had to endure my persistent tendency to downgrade him in terms of his masculinity: I perceived him as a eunuch. Perhaps he knew, very early on, how preoccupied I was with my grief over the suffering Laios. Perhaps he even told me that, but I did not, in any case, pursue the matter. Towards Laios, there was no cause for overt revenge. Looking back, however, I think that the rage of disappointment played a large part in the analytical transference, if only in minute, almost homeopathic doses. I was as uncertain about my inner stature as a man as I was of the physical one. All the years in college I had been looking for a father among the professors, unable to find one in the sound and fury, impeded by my contact difficulties. Now he was sitting behind me, a man whom I certainly liked a whole lot, but whose actual qualities stood in heavy contrast to many unconscious and arrested expectations. Take, for instance, the matter of public appearances. He is "a quiet one", and during the first years I found that hard to deal

with: in the area of public action he was able to offer me interpretations but no model. I vacillated between discontent and
contempt. I knew that the public prestige that he had enjoyed
in the Institute had not been too stable. I perceived that in the
following manner: He has not been able to assume the position
commensurate with his accomplishments. Thus, another disappointment. He was not a writer: disappointment. He was not a
good public speaker: disappointment. He had no position at the
University: disappointment. I felt betrayed and disappointed in
terms of his paternal potency, or that, at least, was how I experienced it. I write this although it concerns his actual person, because I have no other way of showing how he dealt with it.

For some time, the interpretation of these connections relied
on the image of the extramarital child that has a mother but no
father. Then, slowly, the early 'family novel' emerged in which
I had enmeshed him. I can no longer remember the fantasies
about my lineage, only that I cherished, for many years, the
dream of being adopted by the influential and cultured prince
living in our area, so that I could return to the princely milieu I
felt I deserved. That connected with my princely time in the
family. In view of this mesh of fantasy and wishful thinking, it
may be easier to understand why I found it so difficult, for such
a long time, to admit and appreciate the analyst's paternity. I
hated him because I believed that I could not be proud of him.

Time and again, he interpreted it for me: Well, I just am the
paralyzed Laios, sitting here in this chair day in, day out, waiting for the son to return from his excursions and deeds. Only
very gradually, as I learned more about the occasional unreliability of the more famous analytical fathers, it dawned on me
what good fortune the reliability of the paralyzed father was for
me. I called him my reliable gnome behind the couch. His lack
of ambition, ability or inclination to play a publicly visible role
which so scandalized me for years I came to praise, later, and I
do still praise it. Even here there were key experiences to comprehension. I was approached by other institutions as to my interest in a teaching position. There was no question in my mind
that I would certainly not run away from him, and yet those offers caused inner turmoil, primarily in creating guilt feelings towards him. In analytical matters I felt him to be a master, and
saw myself so much as the son that these offers of an academic
and rather premature paternity made me confused in front of
him. I did not want to pass him by, wanted to pull him along, did

not want to hurt him, wanted him to go first. But I misconstrued him, in that whirlpool of projections and transference crises. Once I told him: "Well, it might hurt you to see me get a chair —such a little fellow, lying here on your couch three years old, and you've hardly weaned him off the bottle or the breast." He reacted with the lapidary sentence: "You know, that is just a question of one's urge to the chair."* That phrase was a great help to me in dealing with the tension between my ambition and the manifold guilt feelings towards the father who used a part of his life energy to make me fitter for my tasks by means of a good analysis, or one might say, education.

I have skipped far ahead: those are realizations and insights of the most recent times. Only as I look back I perceive what preliminaries these intertwining processes had, and how impenetrable they were to myself. Thus it was, during the transition from a maternal to a paternal transference—nota bene, it is a question of tendencies, no clear transitions—very important to me to find out, or at least to meditate about, how happy he was as a married man. On one hand, my devaluating tendencies were too strong to permit me to even visualize him as a man in the family; on the other, I had a pronounced need to see him do well, i.e., to have him be a happy person, and thus a happy husband. Only now can that urge be interpreted with greater clarity. I was simply unable to comprehend how a man could be capable of performing these patient and, as they appeared to me, maternal labors on me and others *in secret*, without full recognition from anyone, least of all me. Thus, in order to cope better with my guilt feelings, and because I could not bear the thought that he, in his intrinsic worth, could be dependent even on me and my little prestations of progress (or could he?), I wished that he would be a happy person in the other realms of his life. Undoubtedly all this has an additional Oedipal significance. There were strong desires to alienate his family from him, jealousy of his familial ties, rage because I was only a fifty-minute son for a fee, and because I could not travel to Italy with him as I had been dreaming. Yet, at another level, the wish remained: I hope he has a good marriage, because then he'll be able to give me what I need as a child. A demonstration of the great paradox: no matter how mighty the child's Oedipal wishes, it cannot, except at the risk

---

* One of those "untranslatable puns": Stuhldrang, "urge to chair," also means "urge to defecate".—Translator's Note.

of self-damage, want to separate father and mother from each other or to disturb their intimacy. On that score, I have learned too much in my explorations of neglected children and juvenile delinquents: with desperate sophistication they have enlarged the rifts between the parents in order to form alliances, mostly with the mother, and have paid for this with a defective super-ego, with fantasies of omnipotence that will remain incurable to the ends of their lives, and with the loss of shared parental love. In back of the Oedipal anger and jealousy I found, with the aid of his interpretations, admission to a feeling of security within his family circle in a wider sense; patients do belong to that circle, in a kind of post-Oedipal security.

Now that I ought to continue with my description of that passion, I am bound to err on the side of stammering on one, yet on the side of yarn-spinning on the other hand: the minutest detail of the following episodes was engrossing. Towards the end of my third year of analysis it happened that I had my first, or would it be better to say: I committed my first, or dared to, or was driven to . . . ? It really is hard to find the appropriate verbal expression. As it is obvious that I cannot forge ahead without a running start, I would first like to state something about my earlier fantasy relations to prostitutes: quite simply, I was afraid of them. To me they seemed like incredibly powerful, daring, and provocative women, critical, testing, measuring potency, and instantly prepared to tear one to pieces if one did not measure up to expectations, maenad-like, with callous roars of laughter. The undergrowths of my projections in that direction had been extensively nourished by overheard reports by acquaintances or co-workers, e.g., when I was doing construction work while still in school. A former apartment neighbor, who suffered from impotence, told me that he had become more impotent than ever after paying the required fee, and that he had then been sent packing, with sarcasm tinged with compassion. The very phrasing of the experience reveals that he was relating his mishap from the perspective of the silly little boy who has a great big strong woman take a look at what it is he's got in his pants and who instantly bursts into laughter when she sees it. On the other hand, the braggadocio stories on the building site gave the following picture: the girls engaged in extensive discussions with their accepted regulars about how this or that greenhorn had acted and about how clumsy this or that one had been while fucking, or how quickly he had come just to lie there like a wet blanket. Ultimately, prostitutes caused shyness and fear in me; I was idealizing them, positively as well as negatively. In certain segments of literature that attitude is downright fashionable, and my adolescent heart responded to the projection it gave me in a number of novels. To be plain about it: in those days, the idea of going to a brothel (which did not represent any great temptation, I may add) would have seemed feasible only in terms of the simultaneous notion of going there accompanied by an initiated, strong and reliable friend. I never had such a friend, nor could I ever have reached such a stage of intimacy because the degree of homosexuality it would have required would have scared me off in any case, quite apart from the fact of real moral barriers, i.e., faithfulness to Jocasta.

Prostitutes were connected with my castration fears, and their degree was beyond exaggeration. In this connection I am reminded of a verse of a song we used to sing in the gymnasium which proves that my fears were no solitary individual matter. One of the verses went something like this:

> "Doch ach, o weh, ich konnte nicht,
> mein kleiner Pimmel stand noch nicht,
> da packt' sie mich und warf sie mich
> die Trepp' hinab ganz fürchterlich!"

> ("But oh, oh vey, I wasn't able,
> my little dickey didn't stand up yet,
> so she grabbed me and threw me
> down the stairs something terrible!")

Generally, and secretly, I naturally considered myself a coward and a weakling, simply on the basis of my fantasies of omnipotence and my archaic notions of masculinity, although this was very unconscious and brought into the light of day only much later, analytically, by the "initiated, strong, and reliable friend". Every night when my journey home began at dusk I had to pass a building that looked almost respectable compared to the blocks around the railroad station: in front of it there stood up to ten young pretty girls, flashing their bare thighs in summer, toying with the lapels of their overcoats in winter. I had never gotten beyond staring and shuddering in a manner conducive to hasty flight. It required additional power from entirely other sources to raise my courage and to decide not to refuse battle with the dragon because of premature worries about my lance. One evening I was invited to a party that provided exquisite wines and the company of exquisite, but unfortunately already married, young women. Around 1:00 A.M., I left the party, full of beans and seemingly happy, although the latter impression must have been a false front to the extent that two passions had remained unfulfilled: the smoldering analytical one, and the Oedipal one (because of the married beauties). As I drove past the cathouse, I was overwhelmed by the apparent inevitability that this was the moment. Now was the time to slay the dragon. I thought that if I would drive past, or just stop for a moment, or prowl around the building, it then wouldn't take long for me to lie in bed at home suffering from a heavy hangover and a case of equally strong self-contempt, and then be reduced to resort to the familiar consolation by means of mind and hand, with a feeling of slight disgust. And so I steered the car into a side street, locked all possible means of identification, or at least those I would regret to lose, and the extra money, in the glove compartment, tried to make my heartbeat slow down, combed my hair once more, and proceeded. From that moment, everything had its own pace, irresistible and inevitable, propelled by my considerable preliminary fear. I allowed myself to be accosted by a girl who introduced herself as Rosemarie but said that I could call her Rosy. She led me into the house and into the elevator, and up we went to the second floor. She lived in an apartment facing the back alley, said she regretted that, but it was less expensive. Like a character in some novel of chivalry, I was in a mood of absolute courtesy and willingness to please, responding to every conversational opening she made, but was then surprised by a question rising from within, quite irrepressibly: "Say, how many guys have you been with today?" "Oh, come on," she giggled, "do you think I keep count?" It was hard to conceal that I did not really know how to behave, and I was mortally afraid of offending her. I had handed her the money with the alacrity of a bank courier as soon as she simply asked me to pay in advance, but had no idea how to go about collecting my share of the transaction. I had bought her but was far removed from being her true owner, treated her like a lady, even wanted to help her over the crudity of the transaction by my obliging manner—or rather, wanted to help *myself* over it, as it was against my previous behavior pattern to acquire the right to coition by means of a cash payment in advance. Strictly speaking, one never "acquires" that right when

coition is interpreted as the customary, tender and sexual intercourse with a woman. I really did not know on what level such
an encounter could take place, and thus I hastened to confess
that this was the first time I had visited the establishment. She
was not surprised, but consoled me: "Well, you know, we all
have to find out sooner or later. You can take your clothes off
over there in the bathroom." This provided great momentary relief, as I had not figured out what the procedure was in regard to
undressing. I had a hard time dealing with my notions of shame.
So I retired to the small bathroom, made haste, in order not to
do anything wrong, and was, as I re-entered the room, considerably more naked than she, who had taken her time. In retrospect, it seems to me that she was touched by my relative innocence and relaxed her protective routine manner in favor of
womanly-motherly participation. Although I understood that
only later, working my way through it in analysis—naturally,
another labor of miserable and strenuous confession—I would
like to preface the rest of my narrative with a part of my insights, directively, as it were. Pay attention to what a great
degree this encounter was that of a boy with a being that acted
maternally. There I stood, stark naked, in the doorway to the
room with the large French bed flanked by a small night table,
adorned, emphasizing her name, with a great big red rose in a
vase. The room had no repulsive bordello qualities but looked
lived in, if very commonsensical; it was, indeed, where she lived.
I stood in the door, and at first it seemed to me that my nudity
was absolutely unjustified. I watched her as she shed the articles
of her clothing one by one, and I saw that with gratitude, as it
unified and clarified the situation. In a friendly manner she invited me to lie down on the bed on my back. I did so readily.
Apologetically and, to my own mind, most inanely, yet on another level proud of my own reticence, I said: "I don't think
I'm quite ready yet." But that did not seem to surprise her. Lov-
ingly, she took my pitiful little prick in her hand, stroked and
squeezed it, rubbed the space between my legs, and I noticed to
my great relief how it stood up and looked forward to the coming developments with increasing confidence. Out of a silver
bowl that was full of those things she took a condom and
slipped it on my member. Gently she kneaded and rubbed my
shaft that had by now assumed functionally acceptable propor-
tions, so successfully that I had to resist a little if I did not want
it all to happen in that supine position, pleasant as that was in it-

self. At the time I did not even know that this was one of the basic rules and tricks of her trade, viz., to hasten the process by means of "manipulation", but accepted it gratefully. Then, as I did put up some gentle resistance, she said: "Well then, why don't we put it in, come on." She stretched out on her back, spread her legs, let me move on top of her, took it and inserted it with expertise. She relieved me of all effort. I was aware of some initial difficulty, but she was quite clear as to the proper angle, pushed it in, and said "There" when it had arrived. That was a moment I would have liked to prolong: after all, there I was now, lying on top of her and protruding into her, and she was pretty, and it felt good to rest on her. Only her eyes looked aside, a little abstracted yet by no means unfriendly. A quiet "Well then" definitively encouraged me to delay no longer in the pursuit of the desirable, although there was an element of compulsion or at least of doing one's duty, in any case, of a certain speed to which one had to cleave in order to avoid the danger of possible censure or derogatory remarks. From then on, everything went rather fast. I came after a paltry seven short strokes. The moment of this far too hurried and really not very overwhelming release was comical in the extreme. Once again, I would have liked to remain there, resting, even caressing, but her motions clearly indicated that I had spent enough time up there and that I would have to let her go again. Of course, it would have been possible to prolong my lying on top by asking or even complaining a little, but my desire to please would not let me do so. Thus I got off, once again not really knowing what I had to do next. Even with a familiar partner the sight of the condom dangling from the deflating penis has something scandalously comical about it. Here, again, her friendly routine came to my rescue. I sat on the edge of the bed. She fetched a baby-soft paper napkin and gently wiped the length of my penis with it, not only making the condom disappear as if by magic but also stretching the foreskin back over the tip. My momentary fear that this might cause unpleasant friction proved entirely unfounded. I observed the way she performed the finale of the so-called intercourse, assuredly, calmly, as a matter of course, with great gratitude. She relieved me of all embarrassment, if perhaps only because I was, I have to say it, a baby, and thus had inordinate enjoyment of this kind of tender care. Apart from the brief moments of coition, the entire process had something of a baby care quality: the stroking and rubbing and preparing, even the act of insertion, were all along that line. When I got into her, I was allowed to do something on top and inside of her, but she was basically in charge of the whole enterprise. On later visits with other girls I was more secure in the taking of what was offered, perhaps even a little masterful; at least I prolonged the caresses and took care to put an end to manual preparation sooner. Yet the main tenor was of maternal or rather, frankly, wet-nursing care of the cautiously handled infantile body. This becomes intensified by the fact that no excitation can be verified in them, and the masculine narcissism "to make a woman happy" remains entirely deprived of nourishment. I suppose that is why it is then easier to remain at the stage of letting them spoil you like a child. I can, however, well imagine—and have had corroboration for this—that the aggressive component is a very important one to many men. It is possible that during my few later visits the possibility of fucking a woman without having to worry about feelings was quite an important one. Yet I felt no need for aggression or for inflicting humiliation, or if so, only in a hidden form, so that it was satisfied by paying and by the opportunity to direct the process of sexual enjoyment by giving cautious instructions.

What has become evident so far is only *that* part of the subterranean passion for the analyst (if it can be called that anymore) that has to do with the reawakened infantile and pleasure-seeking needs for care. In addition to that, he naturally stood behind me, giving me courage, as it were, as the aforementioned "strong friend". In the course of transference he had become divided in two. In its own way, the journey to the brothel was a journey to the mothers and their never-to-be-regained gifts. My yearning for them had obviously regenerated itself through him, although none of it had yet become visible in any immediate sense. But then many things proceeded in such a roundabout fashion. Only by acting out and subsequent interpretation have I been able to discover half of my unconscious. And even in acting out it took a long time before the early joys resurfaced and clamored for a repeat performance.

Those analytically well-versed in matters of earthly love have no doubt noticed the way I emptied my pockets of all identification papers, put my wallet in the glove compartment and even left my house keys there. They will also remember my question: "How many have you been with today?" It was quite obviously an inquiry as to my immediate nocturnal predecessors in the cunt to which I too had gained right of admission by means of money. But that too was far from conscious to me, and was uncovered by the analyst in his trusted friendly manner. It is no exaggeration to say that he was really harvesting in those days, circuitous as it all was. Upon my next visit I got a far more drastic pointer as to the unconscious implications of this kind of sexual activity. Rosy had been a really touching semi-pro, a seasonal worker who was earning the money for a luxurious ski vacation. After two months of holding still for it, she spoiled herself with the cash she had earned, and tried to bring her own guilt feelings under control again by giving extravagant presents to her parents. Berta, on the other hand, had exercised her profession quite matter of factly for many years and in a style that exhibited a definite sense of continuous revenge against men. As we walked into her (much less homey) room in that same building, and after I had given her the money in response to a coolly businesslike request, in a far more merciless light, she went over to a closet door on which hung a roll of paper and a pencil and added a line to a row of lines, separated, a few spaces farther up, from similar sets of marks by a thick "day" line, took her time putting the money away in the closet, and only then turned back to me. Mine was the seventh line of the evening. I reacted to this in a twofold way, which once again required prolonged memory work and interpretation in the analysis. First, I was slightly taken aback, at least sobered, by her businesslike manner—or what seemed, then, to be one—and also by the notation reminiscent of the assembly line, and by the circumstantial busyness with the piggybank in the closet. The move to the horizontal took place in a far less enchanted atmosphere than it had in Rosy's room. Out of curiosity, perhaps even out of a sense of irritation I did not yet perceive, I had let her talk me into paying twenty Deutschmarks more, for which she would take it into her mouth. But I have to explain the other half of my reaction first: the number of predecessors did not upset me. Unconsciously, I must have counted on them—to be quite blunt about it, I had indeed come there for *them*, too. As said before, it all happened without conscious realization. According to our agreement or contract she took my prick into her mouth, which was not all that exciting with a condom on, and I did lodge a protest against the "elephant skin" that she had dressed me in. "Three for two marks," she replied in order to prove to me that they were not the cheapest kind. During the oral intercourse I began to realize the possibilities of humiliation inherent in the situation: she took on aspects of a female slave. I slid my arms over her body and shyly brushed against her breasts. She said: "Go ahead, you can touch the titties." Once again she was a wet-nurse, if a peasant one who carries on with many village youths and encourages them when they are too bashful, raps them across the fingers when they get too forward. "You can touch the cunt, too." Perhaps I was the first one that evening who had agreed to pay more than the basic fee and made her feel generous for that reason. But my fingertips shrank back soon enough when I noticed that her pubic hair was straw-like from the frequent use of spray. As she proceeded to manual care, I complimented her on her skill, whereupon she remarked that she had had lots of experience, first two and a half years in Hannover, then six months in this town. "You know, it does get boring to stay in the same place. But I don't like it too much here either. But what can you do, husband and child and apartment and debts?" Thus, finally, a hardworking mother. In a rush of pity, she seemed to me like a washerwoman who had undertaken to do the world's dirtiest laundry for a great deal of money. Well, the wet-nurse aspect has become apparent enough. But how is it with those papers, the question of numbers, the catalogue of pencil marks? I looked for wet-nursing care and for what I had experienced as a proud step forward, a progression, a conquest of new life spaces upon my first tentative purchase of a woman. It was the conquest of a regression to which I did not want to confess in the analysis, or that was so thoroughly repressed that I had to act it out in order to even recognize it. So far, so good. But precisely the same thing was happening on the other level, the one of smoldering passion that I did not want to believe in. I have to admit it: I was also looking for a mingling with men. Unconsciously I knew that there might still be some sperm of their sperm in there, if I allowed it to be inserted. At the same time, that satisfied a cloudy desire for revenge, as I displaced my predecessors in the womb, but, I too, would be displaced in turn. On one occasion, this became drastically apparent. As I drove past the house two minutes after leaving the house, I saw Rosy walking her next customer towards the front door.

This is what I want to call the discovery of plain indirect homosexuality in prostitution. I regret having to use the term prostitution: it carries a freight of morality and law-and-order stigma. Once on the couch I had to wince after cavalierly referring to the girls as whores. I was startled by the condescension implied and realized that I really liked them a whole lot more that that word could express. On the transference level it was easy to figure out that that plain indirect homosexuality related to the analyst as the companion in the joint conquest of women, and to the need to quasi-intermingle with him in the vaginas of the girls. But that was not the whole story. He was not only my buddy, he was also a father figure, difficult to comprehend. And this is where the analysis took a turn in which the heavy, large and fast automobiles of the pimps, parked in front of that house in the daytime, showed us the way to interpretation.

My unconscious must have realized that the girls did not really belong to me, despite the payments, nor to themselves. Otherwise, they would not have to keep score, nor keep a large piggybank in their closets. And anyway, those cars, makes and models otherwise used only by the young captains of industry! So the girls had their protectors who hired them out. When I sat in my car and divested myself, every time, by the way, of everything useful, necessary, and relevant to my identity, I was in fact afraid of beatings and robbery, but also of identification of the kind that might be connected with punishment. True, almost every day one reads reports in the local papers about incidents in which johns do get mugged and robbed, as the pimps of the meaner streets remain within earshot, probably not without cause, or even take the place of those piggybanks behind flimsy closet doors. However, there was no reason for such fears in the establishment I frequented. Yet the fear remained, and one of my snotty greenhorn questions to the girls, repeated over and over, was: "What do you do when someone gets mean or violent?" That did not happen often, they said, and if it did, they just screamed and the other girls would come running, and that would take care of it. My question concealed at least the assumption of violence, and it cropped up again on every new visit, while the direction of the projection underwent a curious change. Within myself I felt a hidden temptation to violence, yet this did not seem to be directed against the girls, but I suspected aggressive meanness in those other brutal clients or credited them with such in my fantasies. The true underlying fear was that there were, somewhere, very strong and punitive men who did allow others to perform limited sexual acts upon their women against payment, but who would, in case of any real liberties taken, i.e., whenever anyone would really contest their rights of possession, strike without mercy. In this way it became slowly apparent to what an extent those visits were forays of nibbling at women belonging to other men, unknown and extremely powerful men. In my rational everyday consciousness pimps were disgusting crooks, but to my unconscious they were males of astounding potency and attractiveness, seeing that they were so sure of their women that they could hire them out for a little money, to let others have their bit of fun with them, while they alone really owned them, and it was only their pricks that succeeded in making their women happy. The unconscious admired those men, which was why the crimino-political day consciousness intensified its efforts to have them persecuted.

Quite obviously there is a multitude of possibilities of encounter with one's own Oedipus complex. There have been cases in which I had to muster a great deal of inner strength to refrain from attempts to seduce the girl friends or wives of good friends. But there have also been times when I did *not* succeed in that restraint, when the Oedipal halo surrounding them was too bright, quite apart from their intrinsic charms. Despite all the devaluative tendencies towards my analyst, he must have had, in my unconscious imagination, an enormous sexual potency, and I wanted to seek revenge against it or participate in it. And, *nota bene*, he was merely a figure of transference in the process.

Looking back, I am still amazed at the instinctive drive that can be released by an unresolved Oedipal conflict, and at the inventiveness with which that unconscious conflict constellates situations that correspond with the unconscious desires for repetition. How would it have been possible not to hate, at least for the time being, the man who so lucidly and with such loving irony demonstrated to me the snares in which I got entangled, time and again? There were times when I came to the sessions in good spirits, full of conqueror's pride or the exhilarating feeling of having found, at long last, my "true mistress of body and soul": but before long, alerted by his cautious nudging, I felt the Oedipal noose tightening around my ankle again. Once, after I had described a feast of seduction in glowing colors, he asked me: "Well, what do you think, who did you really want to sleep with more—her or him?" I certainly had not wanted to go to bed with "him", but what became apparent was the deep wish to "goad him", to achieve a better comprehension of his scientific and masculine potential. Even here, certain subterranean guilt feelings played a part, because a man I had once admired did not manage to go on, while many things just fell into my lap, if I may be permitted that grotesque image.

Is it possible to assume that Oedipus was not full of pride when he slept with Jocasta? I ask the question so as to take some of the onus off myself, if the preceding narrative has been tainted by a touch of masculine braggadocio, and ask you to regard it as a symptom that belongs to the neurosis, one that I hope he will manage to analyze out. Oedipus was abandoned as a small boy child and raised by shepherds. I can well imagine that he was a shy little boy at first, rendered speechless when he saw the aristocratic daughters by the well on his first visit to the next small town. And it probably was hard for him to accept his later successes with the appropriate inner humility. I should think that the narcissistic blessings proved simply too much for him, at first. Oedipus shone in the eyes of Oedipus. He did not rest content until he had made his way to Jocasta. My analyst managed to get hold of me before I got that far, and I thank him for that, too. He opened my eyes for me, and thus I did not have to be blinded. He also saved me from the journey through the ravine where Oedipus met Laios and killed him. He whispered the name of the paralyzed old man in the sedan chair into my ear, and I just cast my eyes down, in respect for his misfortune, and went on my way. More about that later.

Before I get entirely lost in the mythology I have to add something, an amusing instance of regression that suddenly broke through all ego controls, on the threshold of the pre-Oedipal and the Oedipal exactly where the analyst occasionally spoke of "Little Oedipus". One evening, after relaxing intercourse with a female friend, my bladder made itself felt very strongly, and at the same time an early scenario flashed through my unconscious. Almost unsuspecting, I took her by the hand, led her into the bathroom, and peed a great proud arc, out of my erect prick into the bathub; and we both stood there, our eyes shining. The strange thing about such a drive regression breaking through with analytical force is its seductiveness. That particular friend was rather inhibited in such matters and full of powerful shame in the excretory context, so that, had I given verbal expression to my intentions beforehand, the whole thing would have proved impossible. As it was, the occasion was rather irresistible.

Let me continue along the mythological track. Unless my observations have been erroneous, my analyst has had a thoroughgoing classical education. He never lacked in nuances and mythological detail that my half-baked education had never provided me with. Thus he demonstrated to me how I was simply continuing my early family romance in our analysis. In my early fantasies of adoption, Laios and Jocasta often appeared to me only as adoptive parents. They fell so far short of the personages to whom I wanted to attribute my princely descent that I sometimes refused to walk on the same side of the street with Jocasta. If she walked on the right, I walked on the left, in order not to be recognized as belonging to her. The initiate will obviously recognize this as a raging but disappointed attraction and as a revenge for it: in my imagination, I held onto the princely mother of the early days, setting her up against the bad mother of the many siblings.

Much later, there was a scene with Laios in which a remote equivalent became apparent. During my second semester at the university, I suddenly saw him one day, struggling up the steps leading to the seminar building in which that anti-analytical teacher resided, his belongings in a pack on his back, so that he had his hands free for the two walking sticks he was obliged to use. I asked him what he was up to, and he replied that he had not expected to meet me here but that he had wanted to pay a call on the professor in order to "commend me to his attention". He said he was grateful that that teacher took some interest in me, as he, Laios, understood so little about my academic endeavors. Now I am overcome with emotion and very belated filial love. At the time, I was an ambitious brute, only capable of shame and pity. I asked him to leave again, telling him in my affected pride that he did not have to act as a go-between. I was not able to deal with his paternal worry in a human fashion.

For a long time I dealt in a similarly devaluative way with my analyst. I used him as if he had been a single mother or an adoptive father and found it hard to reconcile myself to the fact that there was so little visible pomp and circumstance about him. Today, the affection being secure, I could obviously shake my head over this, but neurosis is neurosis. I do not want to indulge in moral arguments but simply remember my weakness, which has improved in this respect. One may well imagine my gratitude for his patient endurance until I was finally able to open my eyes. And I am now engaged in an effort of reparation.

But whenever my pride was hurt or I believed that he did not understand me, or that he was mismanaging the analysis, or that he was no match for me—yes, that was what I, or the dragon within, often thought—then I would have at him: "I have to leave, I have to go to someone stronger, you just can't help me!" Would it be possible to hurt a father more than with such words which I uttered without compunction? He knew that they were part of my neurosis, yet such analytical knowledge may not always prove to be an absolutely reliable shield in cases where the patient combines a lively intellect with the hurtful intentions of his unconscious. In those days I often indulged in sarcasm and told him that when I would be done with analysis with him I could always go and see Dr. Y for a year, saying I was sure the latter would be able to iron out some of the kinks *he* had inflicted upon me. Indeed, I became intensely involved with that Dr. Y and started admiring him demonstratively; related in the analysis whenever he had praised me in the seminar I attended; told about my progress in achieving recognition from him; but also admitted that there were certain things about him that frightened me. This leads directly to the point of my dividing the father image into two people: the archaically great, and the sick, actual one; the fantasized super-analyst and the reliable, paralyzed one sitting behind me. Soon this division became one of father and grandfather. All divisions extend throughout the analysis, but this last one proved to be the most significant. When I was threatening my analyst with that Dr. Y who would heal my wounds, I did not yet know that he was *my analyst's* analytical father, thus my own grandfather. However, my unconscious appears to have noticed it. By way of explanation: my maternal grandfather whom I had only seen once as a small child, remembering only his white beard, was a remarkable man. His stature, transmitted through Jocasta's unconscious—who hardly ever spoke of him except for a few later occasions when I started in on some family research during my first stab at analysis—became a determinant in my life. I believe that I clung to him unconsciously, despite the fact that he was a mythological figure, or precisely because of that, and if I had to choose a single expression to characterize his person, it would be "worldly-wise". He traveled, as Laios told me, a great deal, even twice a year to Paris, to keep *au courant* in the art world and to buy books. I had heard talk about those Paris trips in familial circles before that time, yet the connection obviously was not clear to me when I did my utmost during my first semesters in college to be able to study in Paris, which I subsequently did for two years. Unfortunately, those were the worst years in terms of my depression, and they wore me down and set me up for analysis. It was there that I had to realize that a heavy neurosis cannot be resolved by means of writing, at least not for me.

At the previously mentioned conference in Rome I became acquainted with my other analytical grandfather, the American psychoanalyst Dr. K., formerly of Vienna. I wrote about his conference lecture and other works by him, praising him, and he read what I had written. When I returned from the conference, I spoke of Dr. K. in glowing terms during my analytical session. What happened was curious. There certainly was some ambivalent acting out in my enthusiasm, and my analyst perceived it, yet he did not rely on that dry tactical expression but said, laughing and full of self-irony: "I'm sure you had a good eye there. If I would go into analysis once again, now, and could freely choose who to do it with—then, after myself, I would certainly pick him."

That little speech had an astounding effect on me. First of all, a connection based on respect and admiration had been established between the distant great figure and my analyst, and secondly, I had discovered in him a small corner of that secret therapeutic megalomania without which no one can get by in the profession, an entirely new dimension, an assertion of ability that I accepted instantly while being both surprised and moved by the discovery that such powerful ambition flashed out from behind the mask of the paralyzed, silent father that I had put on him. That reconciled me with him in an area where I had thought there was a definitive chasm: his lack of ambition. Now, fortunately, I had come to know that his ambition consisted in nothing else but to be a good analyst. This calmed me down in the midst of my devaluation problems, which were fading at the time. I knew that he strove for skill and artistry in his profession, and showed my gratitude among other ways by desisting from my reproaches regarding his unwillingness to "go public". At the risk of sounding a little pompous, I would like to put it this way: from that moment on, although it was not an abrupt transition, I felt that I was lying on the couch of an artist, not an adoptive father whom I would leave again for the sake of someone greater. Once more, a tension appeared between the interior father and grandfather image when I discussed travel plans, to go and visit the analytical grandfather in America. I was unable to deal with the split between love for *him* and admiration for *the other*, connected to his public activity and literary-scientific work. I called off the trip because I was afraid of hurting and losing my analyst. After further weeks of analytical work, there were no longer any obstacles to the trip.

All that does not, perhaps, relate directly to the smoldering passion, but to the problems of descent, of the family romance; to the relationship between fixations and fantasies of greatness, the relationship between love and admiration; to divided identification, to the search for identity; perhaps even to the horror of final and exclusive union based on a blend of aversion and inability—which on the side of the mothers and women made things far more difficult for me. But pursuing the glowing coal of passion I recall that during exactly the period of my most intensive defense battle against a flare-up of my passion for him, my analyst, I struck up a friendly relationship with an out-of-town analyst of the same age who also was a contented paterfamilias. Although that relationship gained its own specificity a long time ago, I have to admit that its beginning was sheer acting out. In part, I was simply not able to endure being tied to *him* with all my psychic powers, without a hope of consummation; and in part, I could not stand being shut out from his family while my filial attachment grew ever stronger. Faithful to his commitment he interpreted this to me, time and again. Yet, whenever a break in analysis threatened, all my insight was to no avail. I had to subtract a part of my attachment and transfer it to the paternal friend. That might even happen on weekends, and especially when we had achieved a pleasurable intimacy in conversation I returned with guilt feelings and had to embark on confessions once again. I admit that I was no hero in matters of constancy, and that is precisely why I have to praise his tactfulness. I am convinced that he could have managed me and kept my nose to the grindstone by means of more drastic interpretation, demanding greater discipline of me, but he did not do so. He gave me a lot of analytical rope, and the tugging reminders were gentle and patient. One might say, and he may have said so to himself, that I would not have been fit for analysis without some dispersal of my libido—I would have broken away. During my third attempt at analysis, with a young female analyst, I became so horrendously infatuated that I started torturing her, merely to avoid bursting into raving flames. *His* art lay in his ability to deal with the kind and extent of my acting out. I am stressing his tact and patience because my acting out was not connected only with resistance, but also with an expansion of life possibilities. I could even document the growth of his magnanimity with examples of interpretation. At the beginning of my relationship to that other analyst, he once said: "Well, well, I guess the neighbor lady's home fries always do taste better." It scored a direct hit on an entire aspect of my early life story. For a number of years, my parents had to go and look for me almost every evening to round me up and take me home, because I was visiting with the families of friends and probably would not have returned voluntarily to the home fries at the overpopulated table at home. In one friend's house it had become an in-joke to expect Laios's late-evening knock on the door—"You've got to go home, your ma wants to hand out the nighties." Yet there was something reductive in that interpretation: the retracing of a life process to the infantile balance under the line, which is always a little hurtful, as it deprives the experience of its specific value. Later he spoke, much more cautiously, of "the grass being greener", and even later about the testing of progress made in the interior, in the outside world—the road to life, as it were. That implied a degree of renunciation, a permission given me to enter other relationships. I believe that it was his magnanimity that made me stick with him. Constancy is acquired in imperceptible stages, and I would have seen enforced faithfulness as a contradiction in terms.

Once again I would like to point to the earlier statement that he had perceived definite signs of a "prognostically favorable" analysis. As I have said before, that did not mean an easy course of analysis, nor easy means of dealing with it. I think that it was a technically difficult analysis, and more than once he indicated to me that he had learned patience from it, first and foremost. On certain occasions it was evident that he felt compelled to *do* something, to structure, to pull in the reins, and this may be necessary in many analyses. But I always reared up as if the spurs had been dug into my sides, and then he always desisted, in his wisdom and confidence.

Something has occurred to me that never came up in the analysis itself. Right at the beginning, I said that my having been in one-hour 'sit-up' therapy with him for a year did in no way influence the analysis adversely. I now begin to doubt that a little, in assuming that the battle against an open flare-up of the passion, and the subterranean and often remote smolderings connected with it did, after all, have something to do with that. As I was able to see him for a year, the consummation of passion never became so far removed to the analytical beyond in my fantasies as it would have if it had unfolded in a state of full transference blindness. I was simply too capable of imagining that I would clutch him to my bosom. Thus, I would not have been able to stand the full impact of the pain of renunciation. He was not, after all, a purely imaginary figure. I knew his face and his body, and it would be most surprising if I had not absorbed all that with great alacrity and greed.

When, during my third try with the young female analyst, fear and depression and feelings of humiliation and pride forced me off the couch and I was allowed to continue analysis in a sitting position, it was all over but the shooting. In the end, I only wanted to stare, flatter, woo and make compliments, being totally possessed by a blind urge to conquer, so that she had to give me my walking papers. At the time I charged off in a great elation, believing that the way was now open to the actual contest. The sorrows of the gawking fool began only later.

In the course of writing, something peculiar has happened to me. I have become intoxicated with the feeling that I won't, after all, have to set the fragments of this confession aside in shame, but that the attempt may be successful. But megalomania leaps in immediately and forces me to make a rather painful narcissistic admission, the confession of a fantasy in which I have been indulging. In eight days the analyst will return from his Christmas vacation, and the first session and subsequent ones will naturally be concerned with a discussion of my doings during that time. Like some passionate chessplayer who carries the board in his head I can visualize various opening gambits. Finally I stop at this one: after a moment's silence on the couch, I say, "Doctor, can I swear an oath to you?" He, after going through his enormous hoard of biblical quotations, responds with that prophetic or evangelical statement: "Let your communications be yea, yea, nay, nay, for whatsoever is more than these cometh of evil." [Matthew 5:37] I come back with: "You're right to tell this to the good Christians, over and over. I still want to do it: I swear that both of us, you and I, will go down in the annals of psychoanalysis." Infantile megalomania is like a stormy perversion, and thus the surreptitious journey to hell by devaluation was followed by the ascension of the idealization of my analyst and of my own actions: my intention to describe his work on my person. It is like a force of nature. Filled with shame I shrink back like any victim of an attack, say an epileptic one, and think: I hope *he* will stand by me for a while longer in my battle with the dragon. After the subsiding of my depression, that dragon is my worst symptom. But at the moment the analyst is far away, and in order not to succumb, and to cow the beast, I bring out memories in which *it* has to feel ashamed for *me*, and not the other way around.

After the episode during which I had for the last time crossed my legs in order to hide my tail, I lay for years, with some variation in the position of my head, flat on my back and with my legs a little apart. Naturally, this could not go unnoticed, and I brought it up myself every once in a while. Yet I never changed my position, I only interpreted it. My courage was just about sufficient to confess, now and again, whenever the crab lice were tugging at the follicles of the pubic hair again, boldly and traitorously. On rare occasions and with the utmost secrecy I even scratched myself a little, assuming that the Moloch behind me had meditatively closed his eyes. There was no telling whether this was so. Often I thought: like a chameleon, he must have a protractable eye, perhaps even one on an inch-long stalk—because there were times when he perceived changes in my face, which he could hardly see, that truly astonished me. Thus he would say, sometimes, when the irony in the timbre of my voice was hardly discernible anymore: "Smirking a little, eh?" Perhaps he really was able to see around that outline of the face that was accessible to him and saw my cheeks rise a little. That was enough. I had been found out. With his third ear he registered the lightest rustle of my coat sleeve whenever I wanted to relieve those pubic follicles manually. Other physical intimacies I permitted myself: when I felt cold, I would put my hands in my pockets, but in view of the undeniable proximity of the penis even that could become discomforting, and thus I would merely stick my index finger in there, bending it slightly to hold on to the edge of the pocket. In rebellious situations I would squeeze my thumb under my belt, and in more phallic moods it might happen that I pushed up my sleeve over my forearm, like an irritating foreskin. All this happened involuntarily and would often be registered with a smirk. One day I noticed how reassuring it was to put my right hand flat on my solar plexus. Curiosity drove me to admit that, and thus he or I myself slowly expelled me from my sanctuaries of regression and self-protection. Yet, compared to all I knew from the literature and case discussions, I was an almost motionless patient. Only my mouth was in motion—and all the unfathomable things that made it work. Nevertheless, I cannot say that I ever wore him out with my babble. I know that to be a popular form of defense, but it was not mine. On the contrary, I often felt that *he* was wearing me out with his babble. I will have more to say about that later, but I do not want to give the impression that he talked too much. There just were times when he found it hard to stop, what with the idea flux being so strong. And he would slow down when he noticed that I felt "run over". Thus I remained relatively inert, which was no doubt due to the fact that my entire body was engaged in slow combustion. To permit it to have the air provided by motion would have meant risking an outbreak of open flames, and I preferred to immobilize my volatile nature. In the beginning it all had to do with my feeling ashamed for my body. For example, the troubles I saw when I had to blow my nose! How ashamed I was to delve into my pocket, to unfold the handkerchief, to blow the nose, to fold it again and put it back—how obscene it all was! When a fold of my coat was chafing my neck, I found it difficult to shift my head, generally speaking, to do anything that might have looked like a gesture of approach. It occurs to me here that I had to move my arms backwards when blowing my nose or adjusting the pillow. I would have experienced a touching of hands as an electric shock. There were times when the only reason for my dripping with sweat at the end of the session was that I did not dare to get up once more to take off my jacket or my sweater. On the other hand, I preferred to shiver with cold during the first two years rather than make use of the wonderful mohair blanket lying there for no other purpose, at least during the second year, after his move to a new office. It was precisely the realization of its wonderful softness that occurred to me later when I pulled it over me for the first time, still unfolded, like a board. What made me afraid of it was an extreme fear of regression, which I would like to express as follows: If I spread this blanket over myself, I won't ever be able to get up again, and I'll die as a baby. After many weeks, I unfolded it partially, thus really covering myself with it.

Frequently, whenever we spoke of my classical rigidity and immobility, he called me "the brave tin soldier". Quite true: when you give the Moloch your little finger, not only does he, in Oedipal situations, instantly bite off the big one, but in pre-Oedipal cases, he snaps your entire body and swallows it into regression.

For a few months, in the fourth year, I felt the need—spasmodically, as when I wished to be embraced during therapy—to roll over onto my side and curl up like a young child. But I could not or dared not do so. The resistance against it was truly strenuous, sometimes even painful and exhausting. Naturally, after a while's silent struggle, I talked about it. We interpreted it. The fears had become transparent, even ameliorated, but the tin soldier held his limbs (but for the one) rigid as if any moment the lieutenant on duty might come by to see if the sentinel was still standing to strict attention. That may seem quite hilarious, and I find it so myself, particularly since I recently had an interview with a patient who got up in the middle of our conversation, lay down, and metamorphosed himself into an almost deaf-and-dumb fetus. As I have remarked before, I do not believe that I had any fear of intrauterine conditions, but I was afraid of regression on my mother's or my father's lap. I was afraid I would become helpless for ever, and above all I feared contempt, projecting it to come from my analyst, but I soon realized which militarily severe part of the maternal superego I had succumbed to there. "Who goes soft, goes under": that could have been the motto, though it was never pronounced out loud, while still remaining one of my interior guiding principles. In the past, Jocasta and Oedipus mutually accused each other of not having any feelings, of being cold fish. One might say that they had frozen, and I am about to describe the curious thawing process that occurred in the fourth spring of analysis.

The fourth year began with my first weeping. At first, that was terrible, but later it became a genuine relief. Of even more recent date, and really only to be explained through the Christmas season's softening effects on the soul and the threat of our imminent parting of the ways, is the breakthrough in regard to the resistance against the curved posture referred to, in the analysis, by the code word "curling up". Once again I tried to combat a curling-up seizure by means of a verbal confession, but resistance became too painful. I could feel it grabbing me. Blushing with shame, I barely managed to say, "Think whatever you like, but I'm going to curl up now", and in a flash I had turned, jerked my legs up close to the torso, closed my eyes and felt, for the first time, the velvet of my favorite cushion against my cheek, and fell, precipitously: into Abraham's bosom. I lay there for at least fifteen minutes, until the end of the session. There was not much conversation, but after a couple of minutes I felt compelled to make a smart-ass interpretive statement to prevent him from thinking that my soul had joined the body in curling up and away for ever. Yet he had clearly understood what was happening inside me and cautiously expressed that he felt moved. Earlier on, that would have caused me to fly into a rage, but now I was able to accept even that, to allow myself to be tucked into it, and to empathize with him. Just consider: a mother adopts an orphaned child, and during the first four years the kid is seen to thrive all right, gets bigger and fatter and starts running around in the world, yet does not reward all her care for him with even the least little bit of tenderness. Yet that is the basic reward of mothers, and the really good ones feel deprived when they do not receive it. Easy to imagine how relieved I was when I had managed to distinguish, e.g., cuddlesome proximity and homosexuality from each other to the extent that I was able to exchange caresses with the analyst's cushion without anxiety. Is it possible to understand how glad I was to be rid of the Moloch, and to be able to let myself fall into the affection of a human being who did nothing but indicate with his voice that his hand was resting on my head?

Desperate and impatient, I had often thought: what is there left to happen in the fourth year? When I felt rebellious I started talking about our imminent farewell, making plans for the free time I would have, considered what patients I would take on. Which is not to say that I was really thinking concretely about my departure. I was playing with the idea of the end, and of the great freedom, the regained autonomy. The unconscious knows more clearly when the hour of departure is at hand. Thus mine knew that there still were hidden treasures and unexploded shells along the road, and that I would have to uncover or defuse them. I do know that unborn analytical successors are waiting for my place on the couch, that they will soon be transferred there in every sense of the word, but for the moment, I am lying there, and he has promised not to chase me away until I agree with him, in friendship and after sufficient deliberation, to leave well enough alone and to leave the field of patient care, all of its barely two square meters.

Not long ago I told him that I used to get angry whenever he let me notice that he felt emotionally moved. I would like to give an instance of this. During the first weeks and months it happened often, and then again, almost compulsively, that I would clench my hands into baby fists, as soon as I lay down, and start rubbing my eyes with them. Seen from behind the couch that must indeed look touching, but for the big boy who was defending himself against the little boy it was, on the contrary, embarrassing to notice with what force such regressive gestures were breaking through. To compensate a little for that, I called the analyst the sandman who was sprinkling sand into my eyes so that I had to rub them. Much later, not before the fourth year, I noticed that I, whenever I found it hard to say something, would raise my flat hands in front of my face to cover it as if in shame. Even this was rather irresistible, even when I talked about it. I felt like a little girl protecting herself against being found out and hoping that no one will see her, only hear her, and only peers out through the cracks between her fingers. In all probability, the experience has nothing to do with the difference between little girls and little boys. Yet, quite typically, I make that distinction because a boy supposedly does not as a rule indulge in such touching gestures, and because I want to pretend that it was an exception. Nevertheless, I was impressed by my sudden sense of the vulnerability of my face. Although I struggled against the urge to cover my face at first, as I did against all infantilisms, I then started to like the game. There was much infatuation in it, some sense of hide-and-seek, even enjoyment of confession after such initial protective measures. It was a repetition of a small degree of magic, early defense mechanisms, early coquetry. Besides, the comparison to little girls is not so inappropriate as it might seem at first glance, considering that I often felt like a little girl in regard to him at the time. I believe that I was, at the time, in my full flowering of the negative Oedipus complex.

Toward the end of the third year, I felt myself with particular intensity while lying on my back. That was the time when I was first able to close my eyes on the couch not just experimentally, but for greater lengths of time, without becoming afraid. That was when I was overwhelmed by very feminine wishes. I was yearning for him to come over me, I cannot think of a better expression, although there was hardly any sexual implication. I wanted to be covered by his might. In my dreams at that time an entirely feminine reverence for his penis became apparent. Thus I would dream, for instance, that I saw the tip of it in front of me, gigantically huge, and up on top, a single great drop of sperm welled forth and I knew that this was my nourishment that would make me well. Later I wished, no longer in dreams at all, that he would cover my eyes with his mighty tail, or perform motions of blessing over me with it. In my fantasies, I was forced to my knees in front of him, and I engaged in veritable worship of his limb, took it into my mouth, and when I came back to my senses I would curse the taboos that would psychologically prevent me from doing any of this in actual life. Thus I became friends with his tree of life and did no longer know whether I was a little man or a little woman. One day, in the fourth year, I was lying on the couch and whimpering because of a toothache. Suddenly I said, as if hoping for a magical event: "You could at least put your penis into my mouth and onto the sore tooth, and it wouldn't take long for it to heal."

Once again I have to remind the reader how afraid I was of attracting his attention to *my* prick, *vide* the wide pants whose ample folds made everything disappear that might have given rise to scabrous thoughts and wishes. Relatively late in the analysis there was yet another episode during which I had run off, as it were, yelling and screaming. Having been out of town at a strenuous conference, I arrived one evening only at half past seven to a session that he had specifically arranged for me. I was tired and exhausted, and despite my efforts, everything was geared to regression of a forcefulness I had not experienced before. After a few moments of silence he said: "Today, you are breathing so differently, from the chest all the way to the pubic area, so deeply." And once again, persecution mania and tremendous mistrust rose up in me, and I replied, with all my remaining strength: "I don't want you to make use of my exhaustion to undercut my defenses." Then I fell silent and floated in my solitary grief over the total absence of anyone to trust in this world.

Because of many different kinds of anxiety, I probably would have kept my prick hidden for ever from his eyes and hands, if my resistance had not been shaken by a circumstance that had a curious affect on my psychic life. During a highly convivial occasion at a conference I had acquired a fecund and lively bacterial culture under my foreskin, and a few days later my tail was subject to a powerful itch. This soon disappeared of its own accord, but the suspicion of a venereal disease kept hovering for a while above the alter ego. That was when I realized yet another dimension of my intense relationship with him. I became fairly depressed and felt, although the suspicion was not confirmed at all, excessively scabrous and leprous. For the first time after a long period, the concept of sin, or at least, of ethical disorder, wanted to impress itself on my weakened superego, and it seemed to me that the world was ruled by a primitive system of retribution that overtakes the evildoer and wants to cut off or cause to decay, the very part with which he has sinned. Thus I lay on the couch sick to my stomach, soul and member, amazed at the extent of my narcissistic vulnerability and contrition. The analyst did not find it as amazing and said that such a blow to "where one lives" can always stir up strong emotions. I was grateful for that manly comment, because I felt like a fragile ninny myself. Full of pain, although somewhat consoled already, I closed my eyes and said that I had the forceful wish that he would take my prick in his hand and stroke it until it became well again. "I can certainly understand that the sick little fellow yearns for good treatment and consolation after having had such heavy suspicion cast on himself." I simply want to admit that that had a soothing effect on me.

With all that, this is what I want to say: I had been a great enemy and fearer of any kind of passivity. Partial successes had been achieved by female friends, as for instance by means of enjoyable ablutions in which I had to lie absolutely still and compliant on my back, covered only with a little bit of soap foam. But passivity, expectant and comfortable passivity towards a man who could at any moment become transformed into a woman again, right there behind me, that was something new, and I was very content.

Sometimes I felt tiny on that couch, sometimes huge. Above all, I was chockfull of conscious and unconscious fantasies of size, and those can be enjoyable and fearsome to an equal degree. All that was subsumed under the expression "dragon", in no sense coyly at all. Often that dragon seemed to be an independent and threatening creature, and for a long time it was uncertain who of us was the stronger one.

One day as I was worrying whether I would ever get rid of the dragon, I wrote a letter to the analytical grandfather Heinz K. in America, discussing the monster within and its possible origin. I knew that dragonology was his métier, and I wanted to explain why mine was driving me to him. He wrote back: "Also cf. pp. 143/4 of my new book." This deals with the healing management of dragons and other early childhood monsters. And so I went and checked it out, in the English edition, and translated as best I could: "Analogously to the incestuous object relations that are re-mobilized in the analysis of a transference neurosis, the grandiose self [his term for the dragon] that becomes activated in the mirror transference did not become slowly integrated in the reality-oriented ego organization, but severed itself from the remainder of the psychic apparatus due to pathogenic experiences, e.g., prolonged fusion with a narcissistic mother followed by a traumatic demotion and disappointment. In this manner, the exhibitionistic urge and the grandiose fantasies remain isolated, split off, kept secret, or repressed, and are inaccessible to the domesticating influence of the reality-ego."

Another quotation from the dragonologist's book which he pointed out to me and which relates to Jocasta's attachment to her own father: "It is important to realize not only that the child's Oedipal megalomania serves the defenses, but also that, remarkably enough, the Oedipal love object's (i.e. Jocasta's) devaluative attitude towards the Oedipal rival (Laios), and the mother's obvious preference for the thus over-stimulated child, are invariably based on a hidden attitude of admiration and reverence toward her own father. Thus the mother, who openly belittles the boy's mother and seems to prefer the boy, secretly indulges in deep admiration, intermingled with reverence and fear, toward the unconscious image of her own father. The son participates in the defensively originated diminution of his father and forms his emotional situation by means of fantasies of greatness." That is a precise description of my search for the grandfather from whom I want to be descended. There certainly is one curious aspect: the grandiose self has emerged in the analysis *without* the mirror transference that one would have expected, and in—it seems to me—a technically different manner. As a result of the strong needs to devaluate the analyst, which find another expression in the journey to the dragonologist, I have never really been able to turn him into a mirror or into a grandiose narcissistic object. With great patience, and in the face of much resistance, he has had to work out of me how angry I really was with him because he is not a gloriously famous man whose very couch would have meant fame and glory, i.e., to just lie down on it, before even beginning any work of one's own.

Of course, the analyst-Moloch behind me nevertheless had gigantic dimensions. This becomes easily evident from my anxiety, and thus it might still be a case of some negatively idealized grandeur. The dragon has emerged during the repetition of the disappointments in the transference that had once led to its frightening growth.

Without wanting to call Jocasta narcissistic, according to the dragonologist's demand, I was still able to deduce that the firstborn certainly was deeply intoxicated at times by the early radiance in the maternal eye and reeled through Arcady like a faun, though not in a state of pure happiness, since Laios at that time became seriously, even mortally ill and stayed away for a long time. Thus, she was forced into a situation of involuntary narcissism: and the firstborn, hardly arrived on the scene, was put in a position where he would almost have to replace the endangered father, or remain his solitary descendant. When Laios returned from the hospitals, half-broken, the situation changed drastically. Suddenly Oedipus was just another extra, a role he would soon have to share with the horde of younger brothers.

Less than a fortnight has passed since an entirely Proustian occurrence in the analysis. I lay down on the couch and suddenly sniffed out a trace of delicate perfume among the cushions. That was the first perception of a woman as a fellow participant on the couch. Otherwise, I had mostly seen and scented that horde of brothers. My first reaction was to say, in baffled surprise: "If you have such a fine lady on your couch, you have to be quite a guy after all." A veritable horse laugh resounded from behind me in response to the way the kid, compelled by the delightful scents, dropped his greatest negation in such a condescending manner. Then, however, there were memories, of the bedroom at home and of perhaps the one and only time I experienced Jocasta in a cloud of perfume, quite early on and later never again, which is not to say much, since I do not have a concrete memory. In any case, there I suddenly had the lost image of the true mother of the prince in front of my eyes and nostrils again, and I vaguely surmised why I had clung so vehemently to that unconscious image as against the image of the authoritative and sometimes hard and harried hausfrau in times of war and misery. It had become split into early, unconscious memories, and the later, never really accepted reality. It was against the latter that I had directed the persistent peeing protest. As regards Laios and Jocasta, I now have to leave a veil of discretion over many matters, but there will be enough to guess at.

I have spoken of Laios in the ravine, and of Oedipus's downcast eyes. Laios's suffering, the diminution of his existence, the decay of his role in Thebes, his aversion against showing himself to the people, his inaccessibility due to weakness, the grief in the background, Jocasta's painfully changed life after shy, initial flickerings of hope: Oedipus found all these things unbearable. It was difficult to love and admire a Laios who no longer ruled his people and was carried through Thebes in a sedan chair. He became an involuntarily dependent child, and Jocasta had to exercise subtle power over him and the other subjects. Only on the high feast days of the gods was he clad in the solemn robes, and the Thebans saw something of his former stature. Oedipus was deeply struck by Laios's suffering and thus did not want to lead a happy and freely unfolding life himself. He shackled himself, in order not to lapse into evil arrogance, guilt and remorse. He wanted to remain close to Laios and prevented himself from recovering, becoming more and more entangled in an inexplicable melancholy long into the third decade of his life, until he finally found his analytical rescuer. During the fourth year, when Oedipus succeeded in talking about Laios, in understanding him wholly, and in truly listening to the history of Thebes, Laios wept and permitted Oedipus to see it. From that moment, their friendship became irrevocable. But Oedipus has never been able to understand fully how Laios was able to endure life, and why Laios and Jocasta had remained a couple.

I have spoken of friendship while knowing that the word does not entirely describe that kind of relationship. Analysis thrives on asymmetry, and that is and remains an irritation to the patient. I have described how I myself have protected and guarded it like a treasure. Yet I want to report a statement from the first months of analysis that was an attempt, an ambitious one, to set temporal limits to the asymmetry. I said: "Dr. X, let me tell you, don't ever think that you'll be able to escape my friendship after the analysis is over!" And I think that I caused many things to happen in such a manner that the conquest of a friend ran through the analysis like a thread, with persistent energy, with ruses and love and achievements. Not too long ago, he made me the first present of a patient for a therapy group. He had had an initial interview with a female patient and was talking about her in glowing terms: "That one has to learn how to feel, she needs high-grade analytical nourishment. Do you want to take her on?" Obviously, one might say that was against the rules, and that the two of us were conspiring at too early a stage. Yet that was not the case. His severity was sufficient to point out to me, time and again, my great tendency to idealize the analysis which ran parallel to the persistent devaluative tendency. But surely he would have to be moulded out of some dull gypsum not to have reacted to my affection and admiration. During long recent months I have been torn between wanting to protect the analysis to the last and on the other, wanting to seduce him at least into giving me collegial advice, or to permit me to attend one of his seminars. Yet the protective impulse prevailed on both sides, and once when I had spoken of his children with great sophistication and my fiendish labors towards a relaxation of the asymmetry perhaps blinded him, quite briefly, I myself said: "There, I wanted to seduce you into talking about your actual paternity." He laughed and said: "Yes, yes, I think I could see that coming."

It took a long time to arrive at this state of affairs in which he wanted to entrust me with patients he himself was unable to take on. He has shared the entire experience of my doubts and internal battles in regard to my outside track into a psychoanalytical education, the painfully slow transfer from shipwrecked patient to candidate for the profession. From a very strict analytical viewpoint the delegation of his own patients might be censured because it introduces the matter of actuality into the matter of unconscious processes. That has to do with the relationship between analytical technique and humanity, touched upon briefly earlier on in this book, and he is a human being who would rather sacrifice the technique than the humanity. One might say that he is not a fanatic of any purebred technical orthodoxy. On the other hand, I have never seen him lack discipline.

As I am writing this during a vacation, I would like to discuss vacation problems a little. The analyst's vacations are catastrophes that can be *endured*, at best, as I am myself doing my best right now in the battle against the depression caused by the separation. Exactly as described by the Dutch analyst Kuiper in an essay dealing with therapists' vacations, I once sired a child in his absence, which then did not see the light of day. I have started friendships and planned projects in order to keep the anxieties of loss as small as possible. During the first two years, I was almost incapable of dealing with these interruptions. They broke in catastrophically, and I was not even able to accept the helpful suggestions he offered, the shared grieving-in-advance that is so important. I poked fun at his help, negated my fears, and I found it incomprehensible that he insisted on knowing how I felt. I accused him of needing my grief in order to be contented himself. But he had a better idea of how I would fare in his absence. However, before one of the later summer vacations I then cooperated with him. I felt and admitted the coming of the symptoms. I was far enough along to be able to simply observe the changes I underwent together with him, to anticipate a part of the pain. Thinking about that "separation work," an image occurred to me that I would like to pass on to you. I had the feeling that I would be amputated of a part that, while it would be returned to me in a month's time, would nevertheless be removed from my interior circulation. Thus, we spent time together cutting and cauterizing each vein so that it would not just go on bleeding, treating the nerves in a similar fashion, to keep their sensitive endings from jutting out into the void. This preventive surgery and the active mourning in advance made the vacation much easier for me, ameliorating the degree of my unfaithfulness and, above all, preventing collapse.

Part II

Written End of February, 1972

I have returned from my January trip to the United States to see my analytical grandfather. It was not easy to come back. My analyst said: "You were on the sunbathing beach of psychoanalysis, and now you have to get back onto the therapeutic cornfield." There were problems as to what and how much I ought to tell him about my experiences over there. Twice it happened that I overslept not only appointments with patients, but even my own appointment with him. On other days I arrived late for my session.

Entirely new themes emerged in analysis. I suddenly asked him when I would be able to let him supervise some of my own analyses with my own patients, the occasion being a prolonged visit abroad by one of my control analysts. He evaluated the question as a harbinger of our parting. The subject of that approaching event was an unmistakable presence in the final sessions. Perhaps it became so disquieting because the old, good relationship had not yet been reconstituted. I was most impressed when he, as I was talking about sorrow, began to talk about *his* sorrow when I came too late or missed the session. That brought a new dimension into the analysis, and I do not know yet if I'll be able to deal with it. It was like a sudden horrified realization of a frivolity that had allowed me to overlook many things about him. One of my sudden notions was: I have been too lazy in this analysis, but perhaps it is still possible to repair some of the omissions in the final months. The beginning of the summer vacation loomed ever more clearly as the termination date. The feeling was similar to the one that occurs when one has been living a long time with another human being whose entire worth becomes clear only when the day of parting draws near.

He predicted that we would have to reckon with phases of hatred and destructive rage, and indeed it did not take long before I bitterly accused him of not having given me enough, claiming that the basic conflicts had not yet been solved. At some point I thought and even said: "There is still such a lot of suspicion in me that I can imagine that we might part in hatred." Memories resurfaced, of long hate periods at home, of the raging against a feeling of having been betrayed by Jocasta. I seemed to myself more neurotic than ever, and for the first time I found the idea painful that the younger analytical siblings whom I was familiar with would stay with him and that he would give them more to go on with than he had given me. (By the way, and quite contrary to my intention to wait until the end of the analysis before continuing the report, I am now writing in order to deal with a weekend depression.) It occurs to me that the feeling toward the analytical brothers resembles the one I had when I went to the university as the first one in my family. I was glad to get out of the infantile dependency, greedy for the new, yet at the same time I felt that the brothers were now moving into my former space, that the parents would be kinder, less severe, that times would get better in general, as soon as I had left the house.

Back to his sorrow. When he first told me, I was as frightened as if I had been confronted with something irreparable. Then I realized that the unexpected discovery of feelings I triggered in other people without being aware of it was one of the themes in my life, although not a very prominent one.

I did not know the feelings of the adults. I had never confronted those of Laios and Jocasta. For a long time I believed that adults had no feelings. Jocasta had a cast-iron ability to conceal her interior impulses. Only once did I see her weep, and that was like an incomprehensible catastrophe. Her inner life was a secret kingdom, so secret that I suspected it did not exist. I can only remember the feeling of great strangeness while standing next to Laios in church, hearing him mumble the Lord's Prayer, asking myself: who is it he is talking to? I never heard Jocasta pray, because she was always sitting in the back playing the harmonium.

Those memories appear in connection with the analyst's reference to *his* feelings when he spoke of his sorrow and of the signs of parting. Apologetically, I said that I often did not recognize the feelings others had for me. Both of us felt moved, and he said: "Yes, often you don't know what you set off in others." After a moment's silence, he said he had noticed that he had addressed me with the familiar *du*, a thing he did relatively rarely when talking to me. He thought this had to do with my remoteness, or with something in me that was not as yet clearly understood.

After that episode, I saw in front of me an unknown, huge space, one I had not set foot in, and I was reminded of Kafka's parable of the person who stands waiting for years in front of a door that is open. The guard standing in front of it is merely an "interior" guard, an interior obstacle. Then, of course, there were notions of hatred: *he* had not let me in, or had not asked me to enter. In his patient magnanimity, he left the question open and did not present the access to closeness as solely my problem, but said: "Perhaps it is something about me that has prevented you from entering, but there's still time."

Now it became apparent how deeply impressed I had been by something he had said: "It hardly ever happens that anything about a patient makes me angry." He had said that almost *en passant*, several times, even, when I had worried about having hurt his feelings. He called the analyst's anger a sign of his not having understood something. He would point this out whenever I told him, during a session, about my anger against some patient. Only now it became clear to me why I reacted so vehemently to that statement. I called it *his* megalomania, was even a little amused and simultaneously awed because there was such a high ideal of understanding behind it. Then again it seemed to me like some cold form of psycho-hygiene. Yet all that was not the real basis for my strong reaction. Only when he spoke of his sorrow did the contradiction occur to me, and I grabbed it grimly. To understand my feelings, one has to be aware of the weight of the transference. Through his statement, I heard the muteness of Laios and Jocasta formulated as theory: "I never get angry with patients." The way I heard that was: someone like you does not release any emotions in me! I sit here like the old pro I am, and as you know you are pretty nice, but my interior realm will remain closed to you.

This is yet another point where cool technicians would find him guilty of a mistake. The analyst is not supposed to discuss

his feelings with the patient, except when he uses them inter-
pretively: "I feel *this*, therefore *that* must be going on in you."
Of course, he has not poured out his soul to me, but he gave me
a hint that he was not unaffected by an absences, my playing
hooky after my return from the trip. And that broke through
an unknowing in me, or through a protective negation. I experienced that I made him suffer. Earlier hints in this direction
formulated in a far more restrained manner, as for instance,
"You want to make me jealous with this or that encounter," I
read as interpretations stemming from his analytical intelligence,
not from his emotions. But here I really sensed him as a person,
and it became clear to me that he had been getting to know me
now for four years, every day, and that I was a patient, and a
learning analysand, and one of his analytical sons. It did not take
long for the thought to occur that the trip and my subsequent
forgetfulness of sessions—something that had hardly ever happened before—could well have as its secret purpose the desire
to make him suffer, a delicate torture in anticipation of the re-
deeming word out of the father's mouth: "You hurt me because
I love you."

It occurred to me how strongly I had resisted the question:
"What does he really think of me, and what are his feelings towards me?" Some confession work had to be done before I was
able to articulate what he must have suspected for a long time.
My desire to be loved and to stand in the center of his attention
was so strong that I preferred to repress it rather than to come
to terms with the tortures of renunciation, or to rest content
with a realistic portion. Yet all the repression and negation had
kept me from seeing the riches of what was actually there. One
of the mainstays of my neurosis was that I did not really believe
in affection and did not know how to give it either. Whenever I
felt symptoms of it, I became frightened.

The painful question remained. Why did the younger brothers, the familial ones as well as the analytical ones on the couch,
manage to shed their doubts and inhibitions in this respect sooner? And why did they, while I was stumbling between loneliness and transient attachments, manage to choose women with
whom they appeared to be happy? I felt like the failure of the
family, subject to solicitous questions and quietly voiced doubts
as to my sanity and normality.

That was the spot that also held part of my fear of the younger
ones, my own brothers as well as those on the couch who were

allowed to stay with the analyst. They will receive something that was kept from me, or that I was no longer able to see, blinded by hatred as I was.

Four years it took, for all that to become apparent, and it became apparent because the man behind the couch permitted me to glimpse a part of his feelings.

Part III

Written Easter 1972

A few weeks ago there was a strange scene. We were talking about our parting in the summer. I lay there stiff as a ramrod, fighting with the feelings of anticipatory grief that were growing ever stronger. Two tears ran out of the corners of my eyes, across my cheeks, arriving in my ears almost simultaneously. Although I had a strong feeling of solidarity with him, there remained sufficient shame and rebelliousness and urge to secretiveness for me to resist the urge to wipe off the tears at any cost. So I lay there and felt how their tracks dried slowly, slightly puckering the skin. Looking back I am surprised, but I did not want to weep in front of him: the degree of surrender seemed too enormous and too frightening. There are realms of proximity and softness into which I am still unable to admit him. Perhaps the barriers will remain for ever. They appear as a raging feeling of shame. If I were discovered, I would strike out with my fists. That must have to do with the painful events of an early, rebellious separation from Jocasta, one that becomes suppressed for all time. Nevertheless, I will attempt to discuss it.

While writing, associations have occurred that it will be hard to admit: "In the meantime, I have become quite capable of standing it when a woman starts crying." On the surface of it, an innocent statement, yet how treacherous are the words: "quite capable of standing it". The next word that comes to mind is "agreeable": indeed, the urge to confession is functioning. These are notions that never occurred in the sessions, or at least, I cannot remember that they did. But this was so in many respects: the unsaid rises to the surface in this writing together with much that was expressed. I am closing the account, and the approaching end of the analysis helps me to get closer to matters that have hardly been touched upon.

Because I was not able to weep in front of Jocasta, a woman's weeping must provide my eyes and ears with a secret pleasure. The relationship has reversed itself: inasmuch as shame and humiliation are forces in my life, they surely vibrate along as triumph and as a masculine power-feeling whenever a woman cries. And I can only ask how far it is from that to an inclination to *make* her weep, while being as yet unable to answer that question. It could be that I would tend to maneuver others into that position of extreme vulnerability that I myself had wanted to escape from, early and for ever. A further association takes me to the motives for my late choice of profession: psychoanalyst. Colleagues are of course aware that aggressive motives enter into the act of analysis, but their routes are convoluted. There are the aggressions of revelatory conquest, and, among many others, there are those of a camouflaged revenge as well as reparation for one's own early catastrophic or painful dependency. But first I would like to pursue another association. In revealing this, do I not frighten my present and future patients? Would I not do better to hide it? I do not think so. I am even able to reassure them. Although I arrived at the existing connection late and certainly negated totally all my analyst's interpretations in this direction, I can say with a good conscience that analytical aggression and revenge for being deprived of my own tears have not so far carried me away. They are contributory factors in a wider flow of empathy, which is not to say that it cannot be muddied by other such additives. The feeling of triumph, if it occurs, becomes modified by other emotions, e.g., sympathy and compassion, which effectively act as a brake on any out-of-control urge to hurt. True, even in that compassionate state there may be a trace of the enjoyment of power. At least, I was always afraid of any sign of emotion in the analyst, although I would have been safe with him. Besides, triumph and reparation do not represent the entire event of a woman's tears. It can be a gift that allows me to participate in an experience that used to be inaccessible to me.

Thinking about the analyst's emotion, it occurs to me that even Jocasta's shows of feeling were easily destroyed by moralizing. To be plainer about it—her gentleness never appeared in an unadulterated form. From these notions there is a direct route to the psychoanalytical theory of pity, which is regarded as a complicated mixture of the sophisticated progeny of aggression and empathy. My analyst has pointed this out to me in several situations, and I am once again reminded of a few moments when it was a question of his feeling pity for me. Perhaps I can describe those later, but here I am concerned with the moments of re-experiencing. When he spoke of his pity for me, I became simultaneously inundated by feelings of safety and hatred, paradoxical as that may appear. I was jerked back and forth between the two feelings. The hatred said: I cannot stand being pitied, nor can I stand the discrepancy of power that has now been created between us. Depending on my inner state, there were times when I was more conscious of his protectiveness, but then again of his aggression in revealing my weakness.

Because the element of unconscious sadism that I encountered in my early years in Thebes was so painful, it took so long for my own sadism, in all its delicate nuances, to appear again. He recognized it, or at least guessed at it, quite early on. His patience may be particularly admirable in this instance, since he was able to wait four years before certain things became possible subjects for the analysis. I can only conjecture as to the causes of the thoroughgoing cover-up job. In the early years, aggression had probably been made taboo more than anything else, and by moral means: one *has to be* a good human being. Thus, the idealized self-image had become purified and falsified to the highest possible degree in that regard. Perhaps that is why I then became such a master of projection. For many years I was able to imagine abysses of bad intention and villainous aggression in other people, of a kind I seemed to have no access to myself. Even now, aggressive fantasies occur sometimes when I encounter someone at night in a lonely street, and in imaginary self-defense I try to save my life by preparing myself to strike.

During the second attempt at analysis, I spent six months as a newspaper correspondent covering the first Auschwitz trial. I had nightmares in which I was persecuted and led to the gallows or the gas chambers. Yet there were other dreams in which *I* stood by the "black wall" and shot and killed Jews, Poles and Russian commissars, or greedily watched scenes of torture. Another dream of that period: I was throwing hand grenades piled up beside me into a crowd of people that seemed to be threatening me.

Many of my earlier journalistic works would not have been possible without a sadistic streak. Books that I would not even deign to read nowadays became pretexts for public 'executions'. Without really being aware of it, I probably even felt that I was performing a service for the public good. That changed as I began to notice that critical articles about certain people or their books were an unconscious invitation to start a relationship, and led to friendships. This occurred during the time of the analysis I am describing here. The destructive element in my criticism began to fade, and I only became really mean when I was overcome by a feeling of rivalry. Yet my book about the school of criminal psychiatry that is based on biology and theories of predisposition is implacable, and I stick to that implacability. It was written after extended preparation during a three-week Christmas vacation period in the third year of analysis, and it is based on a complicated identification with the criminals under consideration.

I was afraid of those vacations and knew, as I sequestered myself in order to write, that the attempt ran the risk of ending in deep depression. When, during my writing, the aggression became almost uncontrollable, I suffered severe anxiety for two days. I was afraid that the revenge taken by those I was attacking might destroy my life. Even worse was the notion that I was perhaps losing touch with reality and succumbing to manic fantasies in my rage. I had to have recourse to a friend, a psychiatrist and analyst. While reading to him what I had written, I gradually calmed down as I realized that my anger had not led me astray.

Curiously enough, I have not yet dealt with the fact that my stabilization began during the one year—during and after the third attempt at analysis—I spent as an assistant in an institution for juvenile delinquents. By means of my identification with the inmates, I was able to slow down my self-destructive asociality. Let me remind you that all this still has to do with the subject of sadism. In an institution, one becomes sadistic merely by conforming to the normal style of behavior towards the inmates. One soon does not notice that any longer, as all who work there act in a similar manner. It is no longer personal, but related to the system: the ownership of the keys, the entry into a cell, often preceded by a glance through the "spy hole" and then performed without knocking, without warning. The feeling of power is so immense, the dependency of the inmates, real as well as fantisized, so enormous, that the initial reaction is one of shame. The megalomania of 'helping' becomes quickly mobilized in the newcomer. After the multiple disappointments, the psychically damaged inmates provide the trusting greenhorn fantasies of revenge and the wide spectrum of aggressive temptation comes into play. The number of ways possible to lock up after an inmate is infinite. So are the variations of a phrase that might be expressed, for instance, as "Well, I'll just have to see what I can do in this matter."

If one dares to identify with the inmates, the inner equilibrium is rearranged in a way that tends to become fixed. Some people remain in one-sided identification with the "victims", and the secret sadism turns against the officials who then appear as jailers and executioners. My analyst has helped me to see the destruction of humanity on both sides. Yet, for some time now, I have been almost unable to enter a corrective institution. That has to do with my memories of the extreme emotional states, the painful vacillation from hatred and empathy to total depression as soon as one becomes aware of the extent of hopelessness that abounds in those places.

The sadism in the institutions lies in the necessary identification with the State's right to punish and the ways in which it does so. Even when one first enters an institution in order to ameliorate the destructive effects of punitive treatment, one becomes infected by the sadistic arrangements for the debasement of personality. Then it is easy to succumb to the vain notion that one is better than the others, because one *cares* for the suffering and understandably mean creatures. One may observe, in oneself and others, how easy it is to set up the suffering creatures as objects for one's pity.

I had been genuinely surprised when the analyst had repeatedly expressed his hunch that I might have unconscious fantasies about beating. He also hinted that he did not regard my concern with criminal justice and its penal system to be quite so accidental as I myself tended at times to think. He told me that he had analyzed a number of criminal lawyers and had encountered strong sadistic fantasies in *all* of them, even though these had often become apparent only after long analysis.

It could be that the hunch and the prognosis called forth resistance in the unconscious, or, better still, resistance to a heightened degree. It was hard going, following the secret twists and turns, and our relationship had to deepen before it was possible to make further confessions.

On the day I left for America, I gave him the part of this record that had been completed during Christmas vacation. The motives for this were easy to see: I wanted him to concern himself with me, to think about me, and for at least as many hours as I was going to pay him for during my absence—i.e., half of the sessions missed. I already mentioned the difficulties encountered upon my return. Some of the causes of my increased resistance (to the point of oversleeping the appointed hours) I realize only now. During the trip, important confessions had been germinating. Looking back, I can only say that I was surprised at, and grateful for, his magnanimity at the resumption of analysis. I had left him for two weeks in order to go and see the admired analytical grandfather, and on my departure I thought I noticed faint traces of irritation and even jealousy. That was understandable as a great part of my psychic impulses would no longer travel through the transference channel to him, but would strive for realization outside of the analysis, and that is a painful process for any analyst who has invested his ambition and sympathy in a patient. Thus, I assume an element of gratitude was involved in my confession—I was grateful for having been received back into his graces on my return.

In the course of the years, he had repeatedly made cautious enquiries about masturbation fantasies, i.e., the notions that accompany masturbation or that are used to increase excitation. I was quite familiar with that question from seminar discussions about the masturbation fantasies of patients and their usefulness in revealing deeply repressed wishes that never need to be fully realized in actual life. I also knew and had finally admitted during the peak period of homosexual transference that there were times when I was able to masturbate only while fantasizing about intimate intercourse with men, sometimes with specific persons whom I knew. It seems, however, that those confessions were easier to make than the following—at which I probably would not have arrived without the strong motive of gratitude. One day, quite suddenly, I became aware that I was masturbating to the fantasy of having intercourse with a girl I knew, standing up and from behind, while she was leaning forward against the bed. It was immediately clear to me that I had had this fantasy for months, if not years: half memory, half embellishment, it related to an actual episode. I needed three days to think it over and to get ready to confess this discovery to the analyst. Perhaps because of the long preparatory period, it caused some palpitations, probably because I did not yet guess at the full implications. The only thing I noticed was the breath of relief, even gratitude, that I heard coming from behind the couch. The analyst then spoke about a key that might prove useful. With both joy and discomfort I realized that I had provided him with something he felt was of strategic importance. The confession became a reference point to which he returned time and again. There were times when this made me angry, feeling that I was being nailed down to something whose full extent *he* understood while it was still a mystery to *me*.

Part IV

Written the beginning of August, 1972

Yesterday was my last session. This week I will celebrate my thirty-fourth birthday, and I had hoped to get married before it. The analytical removal of barriers took longer than expected. The feeling of failure is ameliorated by my comprehension or, at least, partial comprehension of the way things hang together. I'll postpone discussion of my feelings upon parting from the analyst in order to continue from where I left off. I have succeeded in surviving the final months of analysis without attacks of the writing urge. Yet I have to say something now about the change in interior conditions while writing. I am still certain that I have experienced a process that saved my life. I may have lost some of the exaltation with which I started writing, and which well may have caused some readers to wince. On the other hand, my gratitude has grown deeper. In the interim, there were occasions of powerful anxiety, doubts whether writing this report was not an enormous mistake after all, fear also of the degree of shame that I might experience upon waking up from transference and seeing the nature and extent of my neurosis made public; fear, too, to find myself later confronted by a humiliating loss of ability to control reality and embarrassment; fear, finally, that my creative abilities would not prove sufficient to quasi-disinfect, filter, rework the merely private so that the book would reach a level of rewarding communication. Alone or while talking to friends, I also had to familiarize myself with the thought that certain public offices will no longer be accessible to me; that I have left myself wide open to every kind of slander; that it is at least possible, given a change in the political atmosphere, that the book will lead to obstruction and chicanery.

But let us return to the discoveries made late in the analysis. I mentioned the fantasies of beating someone. Looking back, it seems clear that I would not have been at all able to get married during the time of analysis. My attachment to the analyst was far too strong for that, and there were too many barriers still in the dark. For a whole year it seemed that I was heading, full of fears yet generally confident, towards union with a girl in whom I perceived, to an increasing degree, certain attractive similarities to the early Jocasta. In the analysis, however, it became ever more apparent that it would remain open to question for an extended time whether I would be able to contain the old, ever recurring feelings of hatred. That feeling was ameliorated by the long distance between me and the girl—nor was that distance accidental. Then it happened one day while she was sleeping beside me that I was overcome by the violent urge to beat her, to mutilate and wound her, to destroy her body. It was pure sadistic hatred, and it was, at least in the fantasy, devoid of any inhibition. The images of cutting her body to pieces were like a great release. I got up, went into another room, and calmed down gradually. Then the forerunners of that hatred surfaced into my memory: early images in which I attacked and destroyed Jocasta's body with well-nigh uncontrollable hatred, by means of axe and chainsaw. These may have originated during the peak period of my hatred for the siblings, seeing that I held her responsible for them. Yet it must have coincided with a hatred that arose when I unconsciously ascribed the guilt for Laios's illness and mutilation to her—hatred of a distorted maternal phantom distorted by fear and projection in a macabre infantile mythology out of which Laios, too, had emerged distorted, frozen and subjugated.

At this point, and to clarify the emergence of these things, I have to mention another factor in addition to my gratitude for the analyst's re-acceptance of me after my trip to the grandfather: this was the gradual fading away of my devaluation of him as a father. He had now become a reliable paternal guide in my dealings with dragons and similar early monsters. Contrary to my suspicion of many years, he himself had not really been the paralyzed and mutilated victim of a woman. It became increasingly evident that part of his confidence and life-energy originated in his marriage. For a long time I suspected that he was trying, as far as that was within his analytical powers, to get me married in order to force me into a fate similar to his own, one of humiliating domestication.

There were times, now, when he would explain some aspect of his own psychic life by referring to a scene with his children that had made him realize certain connections in himself. Nor was I able to negate, any longer, that he loved them, was proud of them, found himself again in them, and that he did not feel threatened or devoured by them. As I had long equated male potency with literary or scientific productivity, my infantile transference mythology had (unconsciously) convinced me that he must have been castrated, since he did not formulate his considerable analytical knowledge in writing.

If there was a distorted early dragon in one of the centers of infantile mythology, even that masturbation fantasy finds its explanation. But another revealing memory intervenes. Before I started going to school, we lived on the outskirts of the village, next to a few small farmers' buildings with a great number of poultry, goats and sheep. I had a friend there who initiated me into the fundamentals of sexuality. To be more exact, she and I embarked on a shared investigation of the visible dimensions of our sexual differences. I have to admit that I regarded myself as very privileged in this respect, although I also felt deeply threatened. One of our games consisted in my first putting my hand under her skirt and her then introducing hers into my pants. Thus we palpated our respective areas of sexual pleasure. I never touched her inside her panties without some sense of terror, and I contented myself, in the joyful expectation that her hand would soon arrive at my parts, with cautiously placing the back of my hand between her legs, as if it had been a question of touching a still open wound in a soothing and consoling manner. My joy and pride when she held my prick in her hand was always somewhat mixed with a happy song of praise whose words might have been, "Hallelujah, I am whole!" I did not even need the entire fairy-tale world with its Struwwelpeters and tailors with their scissors to plunge me into fear for the inner sanctum. In addition, I once saw Jocasta naked, not much later, and from then on I knew what it means to set eyes on Medusa's head. Pride, horror and contempt were the accompanying emotions. It is possible that I still haven't quite understood, or just don't want to believe, that women really *don't have one*.

In any case, I found the discovered differences quite momentous at the time, and part of my later relations with women became characterized by maneuvers of negation, prettification, amelioration of the facts, or by maneuvers designed to help me escape the inner consequences I feared. To say it concisely: the maternal dragon was so powerful and threatening that I always divided him up into several small ones with whom I found it easier to deal. It also became easier, then, to deal with the disappointment when rivals appeared and played their parts in my infantile mythology as the pack of brothers and the sick giant Laios.

The masturbation fantasy which the old man gradually explored with me and which I had been so ashamed to confess was such a maneuver of negation. From behind, men and women resemble each other, and it is possible to have a woman without having one's eyes glaze over at the sight of the Gorgon face of female genitalia. Another masturbation fantasy that appeared while we were working on the first one consisted of my changing women rapidly during coitus, thus making them less dangerous, and introducing an element of power display into the act. I don't think I would admit to all that here if it had not changed in the meantime.

Yet my confidence and certainty are still very new to me. The pressure of the approaching end of analysis brought to light some deeply buried things. The resistance against many of them was overcome only by means of a kind of panic at closing time, and thus I had the feeling in the final months that the most important things were still to come. In the good sessions, that made me confident: we'll go on working up to the very last day, and we'll get a lot done. More often, however, I found myself depressed by the wealth of the apparently unfinished business as it emerged. All the old conflicts revived again, and they were joined by new ones. Sometimes I became very afraid that the analysis would end and leave me alone at the edge of a dangerous precipice. In regard to the possibility of a lasting relationship with a woman, I developed fantasies of incurability, especially when confronted by always the same scenes of encounter and parting. I was willing to admit that the analyst had helped me in many respects, but thought that he had failed in one of the main tasks, the one of making me fit for a reliable relationship with a woman. At times he hinted that he had the impression that my relationship to him and the analysis was so strong that I would be unable to solve the problem while it was going on. I understood that, but forgot it again, repeatedly, or my megalomania made me feel that I had to be able to solve the problem anyway.

There were attacks of rebellion against the humiliation of being bound so strongly to an as it were imaginary person who was visible only in the distorted perspective of transference and thus seemed to prevent me from successfully mastering real life problems. It became obvious how long certain almost magical expectations had survived. There had to be a time when everything would become clear in an instant, if only he would give free rein to his magical powers. Paranoid fantasies reappeared: I thought he wanted to keep me small and under-age, forever tied to his person. It took a lot of hard work to recognize the limits of possibility, gradually, and to cease despairing over either him or myself.

For a few weeks, even months, the fear of the end of analysis took on the form of an illness. Almost every night I woke up between four and five in the morning, felt afraid of the next day, felt over-extended, unfit to live, and cancelled appointments that involved lecturing or discussion. For weeks I had attacks of heavy sweating every day. I developed a slight degree of persecution mania towards certain persons. It was almost as easy for me to feel hurt again as it had been before the analysis. I had a falling out with two of my analytical brothers who were also doing time on his couch and who are my friends and fellow workers.

Although I hardly ever wavered in regard to the date set for the end of the analysis, all the recurring symptoms and conflicts seemed to point to continuation and extension. Up to a certain time, at least, he would have agreed to an extension. It was obvious that he did not intend to kick me out. Yet there remained the certainty that I had spent enough time with him, and it even survived our investigation of the question whether the date of parting had not been determined by the realization that an entire area of my subconscious had remained unexplored, and should forever remain so.

There aren't many things in my life quite as disastrous as my parting with my parents. Despite early independence, I spent many of my college and university years tied to them by invisible fetters, full of recriminations, unfulfilled wishes and desires, full of rebellious rejection and important rage against legacies of which I was unconscious while they determined my life like invisible remote control mechanisms. Things that cannot be verbally expressed with a family seem to have a deeper influence and to be harder to resolve than those it was possible to communicate. My psychic household was enveloped in a powerful lack of words. No one ever discussed values or morals: they were part of the realm of the implacably self-evident. To talk about them would have been blasphemous, but it would also have meant an amelioration of the oppressive impact of morality, and it would have been frightening to realize the vast emotional distances between the members of the family. The refusal to speak was a way of dealing with the conflict by burying it. In that sense, the analysis sometimes had to exhume half-decayed and already malodorous matter. It was an archaeology of unfinished business.

One day I simply walked away from home, relieved, yet entangled in dried-up umbilical cords and followed by phantoms that eluded the grasp of sane human intelligence.

The parting from the analyst took place over the period of half a year, and I was afraid of it, of the emotions, of the shame, above all, of the formulation of what had not been expressed before, of the temptations of regression, of being soft, of my tears.

It finally came down to those previously confessed tears. I was too ashamed to try anything else, and the weeping occurred only at many removes in my dream. I want to relate a dream whose interpretation was of considerable importance. "I am driving my car, but the roof has been taken off, and is replaced with another, a silver gray top, an expensive one; but at the point of attachment between the silver top and my windshield there is a gap, and it is raining in. The rain runs over my face and makes it difficult for me to steer straight. I can't see too well."

The associations were very hesitant in coming, and there were moments when he had to help me along, yet without pushing me into a false direction. It was easy to recognize that I wanted to combine my own life vehicle* with his, characterized by visible streaks of silver-gray hair. I wanted to remain joined to him, and as that proved impossible, it started raining on, or rather, *out of* my face. He saw another theme suggested in this dream, that of the alienation of my own life from myself by the weight of his person in the analysis. More about that later. Here we are concerned with the harbingers of our parting. He had extreme patience with me while we were working to make that parting a successful one.

---

* There is a revealing pun in the original:
Lebensgefährte = life companion, i.e., spouse
Lebensgefährt = life vehicle (neologism). —Translator's Note.

One's parting from one's parents entails the feeling that one is now able to lead one's life without them, perhaps even the impression that one is moving on in life and leaving them behind. Quite obviously that is not possible without a transient devaluation and even distortion of the parents, as without that it would be too hard to sever one's ties to them. This distortion and devaluation and alienation is the counterpart to the idealization that takes place in childhood and without which it would be impossible to build up conscience and inner structure. It can take place abruptly or slowly. Everyone knows the deep impression that remains when you suddenly realize that there are important things you can do better than your mother and father.

The analyst knew about my failure in leave-taking from my childhood, and thus he came up with an extended arsenal of interpretations and offered me a wide spectrum of empathy. He tracked down variations of the theme of leave-taking that had remained entirely hidden to me. Well, that surely is his task and his métier. Yet I also benefited from the fact that two of his children were leaving home at the time in order to get married.

Once he canceled a session, and although he did not otherwise let me know much about his actual life, he revealed to me that this was because of his son's marriage ceremony. I reacted with an attack of rage and asked him why his brat of a son wasn't able to get married on a weekend instead of stealing time from me and other patients. Then I started fantasizing, still propelled by envy, about why his son and daughter were entering matrimony so early, almost ten years younger than myself, and I told him with friendly irony: "That must have to do with the lovability of their father. What other way is there to get away from a guy like that except by getting married...."

As the end drew nearer, the unconscious saw our relationship as ever closer. One early morning as I was rolling around in bed, bathed in my own sweat, I noticed that I was pacifying myself with the fantasy that he was lying next to me in bed. That I was able to fantasize this meant that my fears of homosexuality had diminished considerably. Having survived that dawn, I was even able to tell him about it during our next session. He was not surprised. To explain my own diffidence, I have to remind the reader once again of the taboo against touch that surrounded Laios. I knew of no tender relationship with a man, not even as a child.

The forms of transference on the couch underwent surprisingly rapid changes in the last months of analysis. What became dominant was a relationship to the fatherly analyst that was increasingly characterized by attachment, affection and admiration. He did, indeed, become the teacher who taught me most in my life. Yet there were hours when he turned back into the maternal Moloch, or into the paternal monster, then into the castrated weakling, and so on.

As I had a female patient who would, whenever she needed it, turn around on the couch without embarrassment and full of trust, in order to look at me and to abolish the distance created by my invisibility, I told my analyst about it and tried to understand my own feelings. At the same time, I started talking about my own never-conquered inhibition against ever turning around to see him while I was lying on the couch. There had to be another taboo lodged in that. For a long time I associated it with my fear of too much proximity: in my state of regression I did not want to see his face, in order to avoid being tied to him forever. That was, quite obviously, mere infantile magic, yet there may have been a grain of truth in it. Then, again, a deeper memory surfaced, for the first time after four years of analysis: Laios had a glass eye, and occasionally I would spy on him as he took it out and washed it, seeing the blood-red cavity left in his face, a wound that seemed to extend far into his head. I never knew for sure which eye was the glass eye, which one he could see with. The inhibition against looking at him was too great, and thus Laios's face had basically remained strange and horrifying. Later I only dared to look at him when he was asleep.

As I had known nothing else, I was not really clear about the significance of the fact that I had not really ever seen his face. The analyst had a clearer view of the importance of these things, and gradually I began to understand better why it was that I had often looked at him searchingly, when greeting him and when taking leave at the end of each session, if only for fractions of a second. As soon as he looked back, I was hardly able to meet his eyes any longer. Only in the very last session our eye contact held for a couple of seconds. I have never looked at a man, perhaps not even at a human being, with so much affection.

That this taboo against the human face, which also occurred to a lesser degree in the case of Jocasta, was now working its way into the light, became apparent a few weeks before its recognition in the analysis, in an incident that I understood only later. I have to explain beforehand that the discovery of the taboo was connected, quite naturally, with the quality of regression in the transference relationship to the analytical father: He was now so close to me that I—psychologically speaking—climbed back onto his knees in order to explore his face, which curiously enough was the last part of his body that preoccupied me for a long time.

The incident was as follows: At a conference on group dynamics I participated in a so-called encounter group which practiced nonverbal communication exercises. The female leader of the group enquired, after having proposed some of these exercises, whether anyone had any other wishes, and to my own surprise I suggested, without having arrived at it through previous consideration, that we walk around and explore the other people's faces at close range. The participants expressed some astonishment, but soon everyone was busy intensely and mutually gaping at each other. As I had had sufficient opportunity to observe female faces, I found myself fascinated by the men. I was overcome as I realized how intense and mercurial the feelings of tenderness and hatred were that started flooding me. I felt as if my face were subjected to forces of primeval magnitude. On one hand, there was an instinctive urge to get closer, but then again I noticed how my face wanted to contort itself into a teeth-baring grin, and I was only barely able to prevent this from happening. Yet I could not keep the corners of my mouth from tensing in readiness to fight, downward or outward, my lips from becoming thinner, my scalp and other parts from beginning to itch. I have never experienced a more intense feeling of a lightning-quick measuring of strength, and after the exercise I was happy as well as exhausted.

The exploration of the man's face who, after greetings had been exchanged, quickly became invisible behind the couch, had yet another significance. This occurred to me while pondering the word "exhausted". I found it hard to imagine that I would, at a later date, have to spend the entire day in analyzing single patients. Yet *he* sat there, from dawn to dusk, in his deep leather armchair, conducting between eight and twelve sessions a day. I am positive that this was what led to the persistent transference perception of the father sitting paralyzed in his chair, having, as it were, put out roots to hold him to the place where he is sitting, while I myself was much concerned with my own mobility and with a multiplicity of tasks. There were times when his professional activity seemed like mere mole work to me: a question of delivering a pile of dirt up to the light every fifty minutes, shoving it up there with his snout. Yet, whenever he made discoveries in me, or shaped something that had the quality of art, I called him a goldsmith who cannot possibly leave his workbench. The one image I found to be most satisfying was the one of the slightly distracted person behind the couch: reliable, attentive, but somewhat removed from the quotidian business of humanity by that very existence of patient midwifery.

One day as he was busying himself with the drawing or opening of the window curtains I suddenly wanted to know, exactly, how many little piles of shit he had to clean up every day, and thus I proceeded, not to the couch, but with some impudence and determination, to his desk, on which I could see his open appointment book, and started counting. There were eleven names in it for that day: mine was the second one from the top. Then, when he had gotten me to recline, and I confessed the deed my curiosity had led me to, after some hesitation, he said, laughing: "Heh, heh, you know, the old man doesn't really like it too much when the sons start checking on how many numbers he's making a day." These diverse images: cleaning up piles of shit, counting numbers, enable me to demonstrate a mechanism that had been a long-time factor in my analysis. With incredible persistence I had negated the fact that he was a highly regarded man, content with himself and with his life, proud of his profession, who certainly experienced his craft as a manly one, although he was aware of all the maternal traits he possessed and brought into play. He was not a castrated person outside of my transference, and even that transference was a shield against the deeper knowledge that even Laios, though multilated and partially paralyzed by his own rigidity, was not emasculated but continued to sire sons and daughters. The image of "cleaning up piles" I retained from a phase of transference in which my state of regression simply restricted itself to the fact that I was lying in my own piss and shit, stinking in the diapers of my own existence, although I did manage to function to an at least halfway useful degree in my exterior life. Leaving the moment of exhaustion aside, and following new associations, I have to relate that the image of the wetnurse in the orphanage who has to clean up eleven babies slowly transmuted itself into the image of the father who brings up a

big flock of children, and does so by means of kindness and justice. From behind the image of the paralytic in a chair, the extent of power and endurance became apparent that was necessary for daily resistance against so great a degree of attack, distortion and misery—and, obviously, that was accompanied by a
rich harvest of attachment, admiration and affection.

I told him time and again: you work too hard. At first, this
had almost nothing to do with real concern. On the contrary, it
was based on the infant's fear that he might not be receiving his
proper share. *That* was what drove me to such perceptions, and
my susceptibility to such fears and such clarity of perception
had been given me early on, by the constantly and consciously
overworked Jocasta.

Without yet knowing why, I arranged my days so that my
sessions came to be held in the early hours of the forenoon. As a
matter of fact, I never noticed any slackening of his attention
when the time had to be changed to the afternoon. Only his
face looked different. During the final year, I had a regular late
Friday session, and in addition to that, in the last months, a session on Tuesday at 2:00 P.M., and there was no actual diminution in attention during these. Nevertheless, there was something about his face that made me avoid those times as long as it
was possible. During the preceding years I had explored his
morning face, had even been the first one on Mondays when he
arrived, dewy fresh, as it were, from his place in the mountain
foothills, carrying bouquets of flowers which he proceeded to
put in vases and to distribute around the room.

His morning face was well-rested, sometimes cheerfully boy-
ish. Occasionally he quite obviously found it difficult to return
from uninhibited familial good spirits to the analyst's measured
silences. There were Mondays when he became so talkative, as-
sociating and interpreting, that I had to point it out to him—dis-
gruntled at times, at times surprised and gratified. On occasion
my need for a calm listener was so strong that I reacted to his
talking with violent anger and hurt feelings. Although I heard
the well-known voice behind me, I felt totally abandoned and
betrayed. The habituation to the privilege of the regressed patient to enjoy attention of an undivided kind and without regard to the analyst's own needs led to a state of wide-awake ir-
ritability whenever he had not quite returned to the stance of
the silent provider of shade, or pure understanding. In the af-
ternoons, he sometimes looked tired, with shadows under his

eyes. He seemed almost emaciated to me, and in my infantile egoism I reacted with rage or resigned disappointment, tending to adopt a benevolently indulgent attitude, not, of course, spontaneously, but out of fear of losing him. If I was in a bad mood, I would say something like: "I don't really feel like telling you anything today. You really seem all worn out." And then I was twice as enraged about the greedy swarm of siblings that had done this to him.

In regard to the late Friday hour, I began to feel less this way once I had noticed that he took a regular little break before it in order to have a cup of tea. In the welter of stirred-up infantile desires, one clutches at minute details. I found out that it was a five-minute break he permitted himself at this time of day. When I arrived a couple of minutes early and sat in the waiting room, I could hear him busying himself in the kitchen. In five minutes the couch has cooled down nicely, the room has been aired, the memory of the previous ass has dispersed. Thus, I was able to have the reassuring feeling that he was making a new start with me. Yet the scoundrel who preceded me appeared to be a typical hog for extra minutes. We all know such sibling types who often manage to have their greedy baby souls come up with a couple of important notions precisely when it would really be time for them to be put back into the crib or to be sent off to play outside again. In any case, the minute-hog before me frequently made me angry because I had to wait longer, and because the old boy, not having had time to drink his tea, would then place it by his side at the beginning of the session. During the first weeks when this recurred I was unable to say anything before the quiet sipping noises had stopped altogther. Even the greatest caution on his part was to no avail. I sensed when he took the cup and when he put it back on its saucer again. Dreamily or furiously, I attended to the sounds of little sips and listened to the chugging and the echoes that the tea produced on its downward course in his gullet. One day, instead of having tea, which I had in the meantime become used to and was slowly able to endure without too much frustration, he proceeded to eat the last piece of his snack apple. I took him to task for it and raged at him at least half the session. Given the artificial inflation of all noises in the otherwise quiet room, it did, indeed, feel like lying next to an ox munching rutabagas. In addition, I thought, remembering my own experience, that he would not even be able to listen to me if I spoke softly, as the crash and crackle of mastication takes place in great proximity to the ears and one actually becomes harder of hearing while chewing apples. I perceived it as great callousness on his part, which had to do with the way our imminent parting made me once again hypersensitive to real and imagined slights. I simply could not understand that he would, without a care and without guessing at the consequences, just finish up his apple like that. Perhaps there were others who had a thicker skin, I thought. My anger was a symptom of an increase in my ability to feel hurt. It was merely a matter of seconds, and yet we have to be grateful for the laws of the unconscious. Such minute occurrences provide the opportunity for an as it were microscopic, final observation of tendencies that have not yet been worked out sufficiently. In this case, it was a matter of my greed for his total attention unmarred by the slightest distraction.

The seven hundred hours of his almost undivided attention did bring about a fundamental change in my life. Yet, considering my rage over his worn-out face, I understood something of what must occur in small children whose mothers or fathers are too exhausted from work to pay any real attention to them. In certain phases, a child is unable to perceive his mother's tiredness as anything but an intentional and malevolent restriction of her affection and attention, and I often thought about the millions of children of working mothers who come home after a day at the office or on the assembly line to find themselves confronted by these psychically starved children, while they really need a little bit of pampering themselves in order to go on.

My predilection for the morning hours also had to do with another observation: around noon, or later in the afternoon, I found myself much more prone to irresistible attacks of depression. It frequently happened that I ascended the stairs without a care at 2:00 P.M., yet I had hardly lain down on the couch and all was melancholia, to the point where I was close to losing control over my voice—a strange feeling, that, not to have one's own voice at one's disposal. It becomes very pronounced in moods of depression: the voice is still audible, but it appears lifeless, alienated, a plaint or a dry rustle. In the transference, it was possible to explain part of the afternoon depression in this way: around two in the afternoon I had been returning home from school, for years, riding my bike quite cheerfully at first;

but then, as I was approaching the apartment, those close and crowded quarters, I experienced a kind of dissolution of my inner personality, and this would have required discussion and empathy. The rigidity of the repetition of interior events that have been imprinted over years, their repetition in totally different life situations, is impressive—and so is the experience of the way they are slowly ameliorated and even disappear altogether, given patient elucidation.

Yet the *Tuesday* depression had other, additional, sources, and we will return to them later on. To conclude the description of those states: I lay on the couch and felt like a soft, formless, deliquescent mass. I was afraid of complete dissolution. One day I then saw this image, behind closed eyelids, not wanting to perceive anything exterior any more: once again, the paternal penis moved behind me, the taproot holding fast and straight in the soil of grief, and I fantasized, spontaneously (and have to apologize for the way this sounds like a straight lift from the most orthodox Freudian textbook), that I was swallowing it, and slowly it became transformed into a supportive backbone that gave my body solidity and structure. At least, I sensed some strength in me again, rib cage and musculature slowly returned to their proper places which they had abandoned in the depressive dissolution. The depression diminished and went away like a receding tide. It is surprising, and possibly difficult to comprehend while merely reading about it, how concrete the symbolism becomes when regression and the corresponding transference coincide.

Peculiar connections exist between depression and grief. I do not want to formulate them theoretically but merely relate what my concrete experience of them has been. One might say that depression is a kind of grief that has overcome the child early on and with great force at a point where the child ought not to have been forced to part from whatever it is that is, in interior terms, taken away from it. In the course of the analysis, most clearly only during the final months, I experienced the transformation of depression into grief. In a depression, something irremediable has already happened and is now darkening one's life without one's having any access to the causes. In grief, one knows its content. During the months of parting I often found myself lying on the couch and feeling the old familiar conditions of hopelessness descending on me once again. But it was often easy to demonstrate that my grief merely followed its predetermined pathways. The analyst was able to come up with images in which that diffuse hopelessness coalesced. Then I had to admit, if reluctantly, that I was deeply disturbed emotionally by the impending loss. This became most clear to me in the image of "walking alone". Sometimes I reacted with rage when he kept coming back to the fact of grief, seeing its clear indications. I accused him, the way patients accused me before vacations: "You just want to observe my feelings continuously to see how dependent I am." "Why should I show you my grief? You're off to your vacation in the South, and I'll be stumbling around God knows where, all alone and whimpering!" This is, of course, one of the analyst's most difficult technical problems: how to make the patient see and experience feelings he has been avoiding like the plague all his life, and whose repetition does not, at first, present anything but danger. At first, I perceived each and every feeling of dependency on him as a humiliation and raged against the one-sidedness of our relationship. Yet there comes the time when it is possible to gratefully accept that there is someone there who can stand being clutched at by one's own ailing emotions, even encourages it—although one cannot, as one invariably wishes at first, involve him in a mutual and equal relationship. The images that he or I came up with for this recognition were quite varied. When I felt good and was active in the outside world, it sometimes seemed to me that I had simply taken a quick trip back to my home base, a pit stop, as it were. In more regressive moods, I felt more like a starved infant suckling at the breast, and there even were times when I felt like only one of many greedy lampreys that had buried their fangs in his body.

There were hours in those last months during which I lay on the couch feeling so heavy and paralyzed that I thought I would never be able to get up again, at least not without the assistance of a great big crane. That was part of the work to cut the umbilical cord which was proceeding apace, despite everything. When I closed my eyes I was sometimes able to feel that I was part of him. Then again I felt how there was a hairline crack in that unity, which then widened to a chasm. Sometimes it was as if two rafts were quietly moving apart on the surface of a calm lake. I want to overcome my embarrassment and admit that this idea of a soundless receding from each other inspired a feeling of reverence in me. I am becoming increasingly aware how poorly I will be able to describe the process of parting, although parting was the main content of daily work for many weeks. This work did, of course, proceed on different levels. The slow disengagement from the maternal and paternal body was only part of it. Nevertheless, that purely physical event is important, as it was frequently accompanied by enormous feelings of hatred. As I mentioned initially, my face often felt as if it had been cut out of the mother's body too early, skinless. Now it appeared to me at times that an entire side of my body had no skin and was unprotected and vulnerable, and as I was afraid that he would abandon me in this state, I panicked or hated him with all my might.

There were more cheerful days. Once I entered the room, and he was sitting in his chair, perusing the paper. Through the balcony door, a beam of sunlight entered the room. Without knowing why, I had to laugh out loud. Later, it became apparent that I had experienced the sudden fantasy of seeing him, twenty years older, sitting on a little bench in front of his house in the sun, and our present had become the past of long ago. In analytical jargon, that might be called an experimental adieu. It was a meditation on the age gap, the generation gap, but also on the fact that he kept pointing out to me whenever I tried to telescope the generations in order to feel closer to him: the fact that his life had long since become calmer and less expansive, while I still felt like "moving on." Generally, fantasies of staying behind, seeing me go, looking back at him, occurred in both our minds, although it was he who had to refer me to the realities of life, time and again.

Whenever I slid back into depression and insecurity, my relationship with him was shaken by my anger at the meager end result of the analysis. Once, after I had delivered a long tirade about everything that had been left out of this analysis, pointing out all the things he had not achieved with and in regard to me, he restricted himself to only one extended statement during the entire session: "You're having trouble getting rid of your notions of perfection." It was a resonant statement. Delivered at the right moment, it acted like a time-release drug, providing a continuous healing effect.

As I noticed my own nagging rage about the imperfect, incomplete state in which I would emerge from the analysis, and as I was afraid that I might also torture him out of dissatisfaction and a desire for revenge, I raised the question of his fee one day, three months before the end. I knew that younger colleagues in training were now paying a higher fee, adjusted to the health insurance rates, and found out that he simply had not wanted to raise mine so close to the end of the analysis. I told him that I suspected I might get so unpleasant in the end that I would prefer to pay the higher fee, so as not to be prevented from expressing my feelings of hatred by financial gratitude or guilt feelings. I also did not want to be worth less than my more highly taxed siblings. Finally, after waiting for further associations, it became evident how embarrassing I found it to be receiving higher fees, myself, than what he took from me. I hope to be able to write something later about the significance of the fee. I had postponed the conversation about raising the fee for several weeks, and the subject was delicate and hedged about with ambivalent feelings. Who wants to start a conversation whose result will be that he'll get to pay 200 to 300 Deutschmarks more a month? That is what it amounted to. It was not only shame that I received more, myself. That was also accompanied by sufficient megalomania and secret pride and secret malevolent pleasure in getting away with it which certainly enabled me to enjoy the idea that he had to work for me for less pay than he got from the others. But then the guilt feelings grew too great, as did the feeling of the distortion of my value system by avarice, and I have to admit that I paid the higher bill with a feeling of relief. That direct expression of value judgment in terms of the amount of the fee is, of course, a complicated and in some ways even odious matter. Yet I am certain that my offer to raise the fee had a positive influence on the work of the last months. If such equations are possible, I wanted to give him as much as I received, and my sense of acting shabbily would have grown stronger if I had let the status quo remain until the end.

It finally became clear to me in this analysis that a reliable sympathy for me had arisen in him, too. One day he expressed it: "I think that I'll be glad of everything you'll ever do." That statement engraved itself on my memory for a special reason. Part of Jocasta's character was a deep-rooted self-doubt which extended outward to those who were descended from her. That doubt was nourished by an aggressive morality that makes it perennially difficult to measure up to secret and oppressive standards. The poison of continuous self-devaluation, accompanied by an equally secret pride over some forever obscure ideal that was deviously connected to "being cultured"—and this had a positive moral value—these were all-pervasive in the family. She once told us: "I am deeply convinced that not one of you will turn out to be as capable a man as my father." It sounded like a program. Against this curse of self-insufficiency and devaluation of one's own person, I had fed my dragon of secret megalomania, an antidote, but one that easily leads to daydreams and fear of reality and makes one addicted to ever more secret fantasies about oneself, of a kind that cannot be shared with anyone. Against both poisons there now was *his* calm statement about his gladness of me. There was an acceptance in it that relieved me of all the poison of self-negation. When I had wanted to study medicine, Jocasta had declared me incompetent, saying that she did not want to see me in charge of other people. That condemnation, which I had accepted without being capable of contesting it, became undermined and finally invalidated when my analyst entrusted patients to my care whom he had examined but was not able to take on himself.

As I have mentioned the dragon once again, I would like to relate an episode from my high school days that resurfaced as I was asking myself, during the final weeks on the couch, whether I would really be able to do battle with him alone. I had been picked for my regional athletics team for the Baden/Rheinland-Pfalz games. Running a hurdle race—which I liked—I was so excited that I knocked over several hurdles and finished fourth or fifth. Later, as the runners were confabulating on the turf, one of the timekeepers said something about Martin Lauer and a new world record in hurdles. That was when I experienced a weird interior event that was to disquiet me for years: against all reason and sensory evidence I was deeply convinced that *we* had broken the world record. But that wasn't all. I had finished several meters behind the others, and yet, for some fractions of seconds, I perceived everything to mean that *I* had broken the world record. As if in a dream, I responded to the group with a counter-question: "What, I broke the world record?" Their surprised laughter woke me up, and I slunk off, feeling terribly ashamed. It had risen up inside me like a bubble of swamp gas, and I was disturbed by the momentary loss of control and the proliferation of the megalomaniac fantasy whose publicly revealed absurdity led me into bitter isolation.

Even now, while writing, I realize how, in spite of long analysis, it is more embarrassing to admit to such fantasies than to anything else. This may be so because they are relatively newly-recognized symptoms of many neuroses. There no longer is a taboo against the utterance of sexual fantasies, but megalomania still appears closer and at the same time farther removed from the rational ego. To put it another way, we often identify more strongly with our dream ideas about ourselves, and thus megalomaniac fantasies seem almost more clearly amoral than any tangible perversion.

And now I have broken out in a cold sweat while describing the hurdles episode and confronting the question whether or not I should repeat another confession from not too distant months of analysis. This one is related to the dragon's final great spasm on the couch. Only a few days ago I still found it too painful to record. I probably had not gained sufficient distance from the flaring up of that symptom. I remind myself that I have decided not to suppress anything unless it would be detrimental to the interests of others.

I was lying on the couch. The evening before I had reread the first part of this narrative, and had found it fairly successful. I found it difficult to say anything, without knowing why this was so. Then I noticed that it was shame because of my joy and pride, the end of a great fear, and I said: "I'm sorry, but I've just laid an egg, and now I have to cluck." The one behind me uttered a friendly laugh and said: "I can understand that. Clucking feels good." I felt intoxicated by my own creativity, as if to say: "How nice that I am the greatest." And I turned crimson from neckline to hairline, and would do so even now if there were someone here to see me. I had been ready to swear that that was the last great spasm of the inner monster; but who knows? I just want to reassure myself, and ameliorate the unfavorable impression made on the reader, by insisting that my recovery did proceed a good deal further, not least because of the work done on that very episode. Yet I cannot quite finish the story without injecting a little theory.

There are many human achievements that would not come about without megalomania. It represents a force that gains its power from the urge to realize a certain imagination of the self. It is mostly based on a maternal wish for the child's greatness, or on the wish of the child to overcome a disappointment over some hurtful devaluation experienced in relation to its mother. There are a number of psychoanalysts who in long analyses of artists and scientists have become convinced that the adoring public, in their cases, still stands for the early mother's adoration that was lost or was never there. After ailing Laios had returned from the hospitals, and after the siblings had arrived, I found myself obviously unable to endure the sudden downgrading of myself. I embroidered the family fiction about princely descent into long-lasting wishes for adoption by that very same prince. Then I drifted off into the realm of identification with poets and writers who helped me expand the unbearable limitations of my life at home. Without the megalomania I would not have survived. I hate it when it plays its tricks on me, but I am glad that it stood by my side when I was an unsuccessful student with suicidal tendencies. It was a crutch I cannot put aside in a hurry, while I hope to retain of it only the part that is useful ambition.

There were times when the dragon assumed scurrilous forms. During the first semester of my philological studies, I underwent prolonged phases of adulation for Rilke and for Stefan George, revelling in my identification with their highly stylized images of the artist. I was particularly taken by the "blue room" in which George would on occasion perform his poems. Whenever things weren't going too well, as they mostly weren't, I would fantasize that I would one day arrive back in the small town where I went to school, and they would arrange for me to read in a specially prepared blue salon in the castle, to a breathless audience of teachers, judges, dentists. . . . I admit that that sounds crazy, but it was a kind of self-engendered heroin that I was ingesting, and in the final resort I have to thank my analyst for preventing me from becoming totally addicted or flipping out.

Another brief digression. I am compelled to it by the difficulty to write about megalomaniac fantasies without embarrassment. I ask myself once again: what is it, really, that urges me to publicly confess matters that are normally kept private? A reason that had not occurred to me during my previous attempts at self-justification: my life had been enveloped in shame. If you are brought up with a belief in sin, you have to feel ashamed for most of the things that happen inside you. Physical urges, instincts, thoughts, wishes—most of these were frowned upon. Perhaps I exaggerated things a little, but the fact remains that the dear Lord, that gigantic pedagogical machine in the sky, oft-invoked and omniscient, never looked down upon me with satisfaction, but rather expressed his concern as to whether I was still treading the straight and narrow. For thirty years I have been ashamed of myself, and then I found a person who ameliorated and in many ways obliterated that shame. The great danger of this report would seem to be that I have now become shameless. If that is so, the report is a failure. Yet I want to tell you about the process, the gradual dissolution of shame, without stopping short of the point where I can still feel acute embarrassment. It is utopian to imagine that anyone could ever be entirely free of shame; but it would seem useful to overcome an oppressive surplus of shame, something artists frequently manage to do. No doubt about it: I am so grateful for the analysis that I am not yet quite able to keep my missionary urge in check.

Before relating a few more instances of megalomania, I'll try to explain why some of these only came to full fruition in the last months of analysis and thus accessible to therapeutic scrutiny and treatment. As we now know, primarily thanks to Heinz Kohut*, the therapeutically revelent appearance of megalomania fantasies is related to certain very early mother-child relationships and their reflection in forms of transference. Regressing, the patient becomes, once again, either part of the analyst, or mirrors himself in the analyst, or experiences him as another who is similar to him, in whom he can rediscover himself. Such forms of transference presuppose a disturbance in the development of the self, the inmost kernel of personality, on which our self-respect and self-love is based if it has been sufficiently nourished by the "gleam in mother's eye". During the first years of analysis, however, I had strongly devaluated my analyst, exactly because of my megalomania, and had deprived him of many traits that would have been a help in idealizing his person. I certainly loved him but admired *others*, perhaps even despised him a little, as a hired wet-nurse. Admiration really unfolded only in the last year of analysis, at that point no longer in terms of blind transference and attribution of magical powers, but in terms of my more exact observation of his skill, the dismantling of negative transference and all the revengeful devaluations. In terms of the family novel (and he often used this image), my analyst's role was that of the unwed mother who raises the child in spite of being officially urged to have an abortion—paying the high price that the child does not find the glorious father it goes out to look for.

---

* Heinz Kohut, *Analysis of Self*. New York: International Universities Press, 1971.

One allows oneself to be fed and cleaned by an unwed, little-respected mother or by a hired wet-nurse; but her lap does not provide sufficient nourishment for dreams, for idealization and shared illusions of grandeur. I suffered from a genuine disturbance of that vital ability to idealize. My relationship to others was characterized by the inability to see them in positive terms. Only in the last year of analysis, perhaps even a little earlier, as I experienced while conducting my own treatment of patients the reliability of what I had experienced with and learned from him, did I put an end to my devaluation of my analyst. He was, now, great enough in my fantasies: I was able to pull up the deep roots of those weeds.

One of the fantasies that kept tormenting me long into my days as a graduate student was feeling disturbed by every news item that recorded some remarkable achievement by someone else my age. I was hurt by it and easily depressed. References to the youngest college professor, the youngest mayor, secretary of state, etc., were enough to throw me off balance. In my daydreams I fantasized that I would soon be whisked away from my seminar seat to some important position, and thus my true worth would be revealed at long last. At the time of the coronation of King Constantine of Greece, at the beginning of the sixties—during my second attempt to be analyzed—I said, quite seriously, while obviously in a state of regression:"A coronation, that would be the thing for me—I could really show them who I am." When de Gaulle retired, I dreamt that I had to take an important message to him, bearing it on a velvet cushion. *He* was, after all, a little greater than I was. For a long time I lacked confidence to relate such fantasies to the analyst, although I had already told him the most embarrassing sexual fantasies long ago. First of all, I clung to the notion that he was just good enough to liberate me from my depression. Secondly, I did not believe that he would be able to appreciate those illusions of grandeur, since I had decided that he was a pitiful petty bourgeois quite incapable of thinking in ways suited to the dimensions of my grandiose self. On the other hand, there always is some fear *for* one's megalomania, and this can be just as strong as the fear of castration. While I still was the unsuccessful student, in the first year of analysis, I really did need it as a crutch.

Thus camouflaged by theoretical overgrowth I can now proceed to discuss that episode some more. I was lying on the couch and had to burst out clucking over my half-laid egg. As I noticed that the climate in back of the couch was favorable, I gave into my fantasies, and these proceeded approximately thus: "It's really wild that so many people will get to read this book. Thousands of patients lying on their couches. And that is why all the analysts will have to read it too. They won't be too happy about it. Strange to think that there will be talk about me in so many analyses. For some time, the book will change the analytical situation in many cases. Perhaps it will be translated and published in America. All the aspiring psychotherapists in the world will read it. It really changes the whole idea of psychoanalysis, at least by a couple of millimeters. Well, Freud was pretty megalomaniacal himself. I'd like to write a book about that some time: 'Freud's Megalomania'. They've just been too cowardly to tackle the subject." From behind the couch: "Freud was able to make his megalomania come true." I did not want to be sidetracked and responded merely by: "Right." Then there was a silence—a silence for shame. I went on: "Well, anyway, I should be getting the Nobel Prize sometime, soon if possible." Silence. Red ears. Accelerated heartbeat. From behind, an oracular "Uh-huh". Another silence. My forehead turned dewy, I was sweating, but I *had* gotten it off my chest, that deeply buried adolescent fantasy. Imperceptibly to oneself, such fantasies can cause considerable disarray in the psychic household, first by their tendency to devaluate the reality that is accessible by means of actual achievement, and also by the temptation to resolve difficulties and disappointments by simply retreating into the dream world, whence one then hurls ineffectual thunderbolts of contempt at all the others.

Such a confession on the couch, made at the right moment, is like lancing a deep-seated boil to drain off pus and poison. The healing can begin.

Nothing is a better antidote to megalomania than to become a working analyst oneself. Like many beginners, perhaps a little more so, I believed that I would be able to cure patients twice as fast as anybody else. *I* have been cured of that belief. No magic works on your average solid resistance, and if one is deceived by a rapid transference "cure", one ends up working a few months' overtime behind the couch. The daily patience required for my own psychological microscopy of my own patients provided a bridge over to admiration of my analyst—which was what finally made those swamp flowers burst into bloom. As I had tried to negate my descent from my true parents in my family fantasies, I had also tried to negate that of my analyst. He chose to use the analytical 'family romance' while interpreting his transference position. After the one-to-one relationship to the unmarried mother had been transcended and a measure of paternality had become evident, he based this on a part of the Oedipus myth that is little used otherwise. There was that shepherd and his wife, surrogates for the unknown royal parents, who found the abandoned infant in the mountains and brought him up. That position allowed my megalomania to express itself in a friendly fashion. One does have a father as soon as one manages to concentrate affection and admiration upon *one* man for a sufficient length of time. I spent a few years being hurt because I did not find anything to admire in him, and took revenge for that feeling, until I discovered his humanity, his ability to stay patiently in the background, until I had done dreaming.

As the secret mania began to fade, it became possible for me to get along better with other men who were possible competitors. One of them even told me: "Well, it's getting quite bearable to be around you." I was able to associate with men without having to measure up to them continuously and without becoming paralyzed by undisguised fears of homosexuality or becoming aggressive out of the tensions of rivalry. The sessions began to provide more and more situations that had both of us laughing out loud. After it had become relatively clear that I would no longer enter matrimony while still being attached to the umbilical cord, and after I was better able, towards the end, to face the fact that I had entered into an attachment to him that did, to some extent, diminish the intensity of other possible attachments, there arose the question what I would do with the freed libido after the end of the analysis. There were times when I found it humiliating and unfair to a possible partner to think that I would enter into an attachment in response to the pressure caused by the cutting of the cord. As we know, the analysts simply did not allow their patients to either get married or divorced while they were in analysis. Freud makes the laconic remark that most patients did not waste much time before getting married after the conclusion of treatment. I expect that to be the case with me as well. My analyst did not acquire any perpetual rights on my urge to attachment. On the contrary, there are many aspects of a voluntary attachment that I only discovered through him.

During the last months, with their frequent mention of parting, male friendships grew stronger, and I even formed new ones. Quite gradually I had become capable of friendship and affection.

One day as I was lying on the couch, positively trembling with newly-liberated affection, I said to him: "When I stop coming here, I guess I'll fall victim to the *furor pseudopodicus* —what I mean is, I expect to get a bad case of the matrimonial urge." He uttered a thoughtful "uh-huh", and then, with delicate irony: "Yes, yes, my little paramecium." Amoeba-fashion, the libidinous pseudopods are able to extend and retract the self: but he introduced the amoeba's *prey* into the picture, the paramecium.* There was much unforced laughter at that. With his help, my fear of dragons had diminished considerably, and thus his prediction no longer seemed like an invitation into a trap.

Towards the end, when I seemed to be forming an exaggerated number of friendly acquaintanceships with other men his age, he said: "There seem to be quite serious problems of redistribution." And after I felt guilty and wanted to swear eternal loyalty, he told me the story of the widow of Ephesus, for my edification and the relief of my conscience, but also, it seemed to me after some thought about it, in some measure for his own consolation: "A young widow sits weeping, fit to break one's heart, at the graveside of her husband who has just been buried. A guard whose duty it is to watch over a gallows to prevent a recently hanged man's relatives from cutting him down and thus to preserve him *pour encourager les autres*, hears her crying, listens to her tale of woe, starts consoling her, and she lets herself be consoled, and soon neither of them pays too much attention to anything else. When the guard returns to his post, he finds the hanged man gone. He becomes scared, does not know what to do. But the widow is so delighted with his powers of consolation that she makes him a gift of her husband's corpse, and they proceed to string it up in the other man's stead. Then they happily walk off together."

Such a story does of course constitute a most provocative interpretation, and it presupposes a relatively intimate degree of acquaintance. Nevertheless, I became furious about the cynical

---

* This is the sense of the German original, although the latter makes its point by means of a pun. In German, the paramecium is *das Pantoffeltier*, and a hen-pecked male is known as a *Pantoffelheld*—a "bedroom slipper hero." Paramecia have no pseudopods; amoebae do.—Translator's note.

reduction of my feelings that it seemed to indicate at first, and I asked, full of venom: "And which one of us is the widow?" In my parting grief, the professionalism of our relationship—despite its being supported by mutual sympathy—became, once again, almost grotesquely apparent to me. At least to the extent that the departing patient wishes, the way a child would, that its mother does not immediately acquire another child as soon as the first one has walked out of the house, or: that the analyst does not instantly replace him on the couch without a period of mourning. I knew that a great number of patients and student analysts were waiting for my place. The bitter truth is that the gaps have to be closed quickly. The story had been directed at me, not at him. It was a reminder that disloyalty may be a healthy way of dealing with some moments that seem to demand eternal loyalty, because it is hard to make a life out of memories and fragments of transference.

As the work on parting seemed, on the whole, painful to me, and I became afraid of the deepening of feelings and the chaotic seesawing between hatred and affection, I had to resist the strong tempation simply to stop going. This happened in the final weeks. It is a way of ending the analysis that is quite popular among patients: to leave the analyst without saying goodbye, thus proving their own autonomy and independence to themselves. I was afraid of a recurring fantasy: at the very moment of parting, at least, I wanted to embrace him—but I feared that I might lose control of my emotions and thus do something that would cause both of us embarrassment.

From a certain moment, reflections on the mode of parting became quite prominent. Beginning therapy, I had spent a year sitting in a chair facing him, and intended to do so again at the end, at least for a while. Four weeks before the vacation, as the time to rise from the couch drew closer, I realized how difficult it would be. The following scene seemed to be the best approximation. The room is dark. You have just had intimate intercourse with a woman, without really being able to see her. Now you are supposed to switch on the light, and you will see each other, and put on your clothes, and together you'll straighten out the rumpled bed, and then you are supposed to talk to each other, face to face, discussing what it has all been about. Four weeks before the end proved to be too soon for me. Then I decided I'd do it in two weeks from that day. Finally, it amounted to the five days of the last week. He let me decide.

I still have to explain the previously mentioned 'Tuesday depression' a little more. Tuesdays at two o'clock in the afternoon, on the couch, I used to become deeply depressed, with surprising regularity. I thought it had all been in vain. I was still as sick as ever. I connected that with the time of day of my return from school, and I am sure that is correct. Then, however, it became apparent that something else played a part. On Tuesday mornings, I had a control session with that Dr. Y, my analyst's analytical father, and for a time he appeared to me as an archaically stern and powerful man, ruling the empire of the unconscious like the Green Man rules the dark forest. He combined, or rather, I combined in him all the traits of never-experienced powerful paternality, including the ability to sustain absolute adherence to whatever has been recognized as right. For several months I would have the feeling, once a week, that I had encountered a man in these intimate pedagogical circumstances whose massive austerity presented a challenge to me, with whom I had to struggle to be able to go on my way, the outcome being uncertain. For a few months, he was Laios *before* his illness, a great figure who seemed powerful enough to break one's back in two if one grew faint while wrestling with him. A submerged dimension of masculinity appeared there, one that I had done without. Once more its absence caused me grief. That archaic paternality had never been achieved at any point of transference with my analyst. Although it was integrated into the adult reality of analytical training, it still was an excursion back into the realm of phantoms. My depression was a transitory outburst of a deep-seated deprivation experienced in a time when sons otherwise see their fathers as dangerous and admired giants. Laios was a broken giant, this man an unbroken one, and thus he set a part of scarred and incomplete psychic structure in motion again. The child's buried wish for a powerful father revived for a moment, and as my analyst was well aware of it all, he chose a term for this violent subsidiary transference: he called it "complimentary". A wound that had not closed during my time with him was now healing some—because of my contact with another man—and that Tuesday depression gradually changed into a Tuesday identification with Dr. Y, from whom I have learned so much.

All this leads me to the question to what extent an analytical dependency on another person, experienced in the course of of many hundreds of hours, influences one's own life. How free is one to pursue one's own development? One of the most frequently marshaled arguments against psychoanalysis is exactly that dependency one gets "forced" into and that is seen as an illegitimate tool for change, as manipulation, as vulnerable and humiliating infantilization. Naturally I believe, today, that I am more myself than I ever was before. How to make that credible? It could be a delusion, a flattering fiction devised to prettify what was a state of subjection. One's own vulnerability on the couch appears enormous, and some projections by patients really make one feel like a tyrant enthroned high above the clouds who might be powerful enough to destroy them, or like a massive monster that is paralyzing them, or like a patient and sophisticated trapper who tries to capture their souls. Without exaggeration, I can say that next to his patience, my analyst's most significant characteristic was his ability to respect my freedom. Quite frequently, this is what causes trouble. The patient wants and strives for guidance and gets upset by the distance, by the absence of a pedagogical takeover. Only after he feels his own powers gradually growing again does he comprehend with gratitude that he could not have been guided by "advice". One might say that the basic supporting hypothesis of an analysis is the assumption that the patient is unique, although that uniqueness is undeveloped or has been hampered in its development. The analyst works for a realization of that potential, and that is the utopian aspect of the analysis.

Repeatedly, and especially towards the end, my analyst pointed out the problem of a possible over-alienation of my person. When, in those final weeks, I once engaged in silent contemplation of the past four and a half years, he quoted two lines from Schubert's *Winterreise*: *Fremd bin ich eingezogen, fremd zieh ich wieder aus.** It was one of those irritant interpretations, as I would like to call them, in which a pointed, jagged sentence is introduced into a still chaotic but active field, creating a stir, encouraging clarification. The question is: into which, or into how many, of one's own areas of life does the identification with the analyst extend? Naturally, that will also depend on the extent that the analyst is able to control his secret need to be and to remain a central figure in the patient's life. If transference does not unfold forcefully, the potential healing process remains a shallow one. If the analyst should prove unable to restrain himself

---

* "A stranger I arrived in town, and as a stranger leave."

entirely in his wish to focus the patient's most essential emotions on himself, the result could be an attachment whose dissolution is hampered either by the analyst's narcissism or by other unresolved problems. My identification with him was a fragmentary one from the very beginning: there were too many areas in which he was not a possible example for me. The split in identification remained quite painful throughout the analysis. For a long time, my attitude towards him was tainted by contempt and devaluation. The extent of his social and political reclusiveness always remained incomprehensible to me. I hardly ever talked politics with him, being afraid of alienation or conflict. One might say that politics was the only taboo between us that both parties respected. I considered him a moderate or conservative liberal. He did not, finally, believe in the possibility of changing the world or people except by means of patient, analytical tinkering. As a sociologist, I tended to regard his ideas, presented *en passant,* on the functioning of society as naive and reductionist in the psychological sense. *He* probably regarded me as a half-domesticated *Sturm und Drang* person in whom cautious little signs of maturation, wisdom and humor were beginning to appear. It is possible that I became, during this analysis, more resigned or more realistic in regard to the transmutability of the world; but this may just as well have to do with painful experiences in my advisory dealings with social institutions.

During the very last session, as he was finally releasing me into my very own existence, he told me, bequeathed to me, as it were, a story that summed up his attitude towards my freedom: "A warden in a large wildlife reservation had come across an orphaned lion cub. He raised it with a bottle, and the lion got really used to him, allowed him to feed him, and tended to be quite tame. The warden was tempted by the idea of having a lion as a pet, but he remembered that lions are born to a life in the wild. Thus he decided to go out with the lion and to practice the stalking and killing of prey with him until the deformed instincts returned to their species-specific channels. Then, one day, when the lion was fully grown, he left the lion in the veldt, and thereafter he would run into him every couple of months or so on his rounds: every time, the lion would walk up to him for a while, but be on its way again a little later." The story took my breath away and made a curiously strong impression. It was the hour of parting. But I also discovered, almost reluctantly, and a little embarrassed by such superstitious proclivities, how strongly I had become identified with my zodiacal sign. The lion story was a part of my infantile mythology without his having known that, and once again, in the last minutes, I felt *understood* to a rare degree.

Before the final hour, which I intended to pass in the horizontal position, he kept me waiting for nine minutes past the appointed time. When the character before me finally took off, my analyst did not utter a word of apology. The previous day he had informed me that the very last session would probably have to be cancelled because of his travel preparations. I was able to take that, but those nine minutes proved unbearable. I arrived feeling solemn and, although I was almost five years old and psychically almost ready to start grade school, I assumed in my regression that he would be similarly disposed, so that the extent of what was going on with him and me would not really permit of any delays. Thus I lay on the couch, feeling resentful and rebellious, swearing to myself: I won't say a word to that brutal bastard. It was easy to keep this up for fifteen minutes. He dropped one or two ridiculous "Uh-uh" 's, quite insufficient to bring me out of my vengeful brooding. Then I began to realize that the cost of that brooding began to seem too high. But I found no way to bridge the gap in one go. Yet my thoughts were darting to and fro, and it occurred to me how I had often used small pretexts, before vacations, to ease the pain of parting by such resentment. I recalled a series of earlier interpretations of my particular ability to cause guilt feelings in others after they had offended me. Finally, I remembered the parting maneuvers I was experiencing with a patient of my own, and then I had to laugh and say: "Yesterday I was telling a female patient who started complaining and accusing me of callousness in her next-to-last session before the vacation: 'Well, you see, its easier to say goodbye to an asshole.'" He, too, had to laugh, and there was a great deal of satisfaction for him in my gradual re-emergence from a sulk, managed by means of associations, distancing, comparison, self-irony, and other ingredients. He said: "I was just sitting there and watching you clamber up out of a deep pit, *all by yourself*—and I really felt very pleased and contented." Such moments reassured me in my repeated moments of doubts about the outcome of the analysis, and it became easier to distinguish what had been achieved from what was left for me to do by myself without his help.

The last hours sitting up were spent in a mutual summing-up. That does, of course, sound easier than it was. I had not really made it quite clear to him that I wanted to sit the last five hours, and as I, half rebellious, half embarrassed, took my place in one of the chairs that stood facing the couch, he had to work his way up out of the deep leather armchair behind the couch to come and join me. Now there were the problems of looking at each other. I am really quite good at observing others surreptitiously, and I am sure he is too. Thus, neither one of us wanted to offend the other by direct stares, and we went through a rigmarole of looking, and then looking away, and smiling, until I was able to grasp and express the first coherent thought. But as soon as I started talking, we were back on solid ground, and we had five hours of serious conversation between men who have successfully completed a long task together.

I asked him about technical problems in my analysis, and he replied readily. To the question if it had not been almost unbearable to deal with me at times, and how he had been able to stand it, he replied: "Yes, right at the beginning—your way of becoming terribly hurt given the least excuse: that was pretty hard to take at times. You were covered by open wounds. I had to feel guilty so often, and no one likes that. Sometimes I just had to dive for cover to get out of the line of fire." He went on to meditate a little about the difference between anger and blind rage, saying that anger was closer to the self, also closer to a possible real justification, already-filtered rage, as it were—closer to reality and thus accessible to treatment. Rage, on the other hand, was almost directionless, and existed outside of a visible relationship between cause and emotional catastrophe. He told me that as soon as he noticed that my fits of rage were transitional forms in the direction of anger, he felt reassured and able to stand them despite their corrosiveness, which was due to my frequently perfidious language games. He said he had found it helpful to remember something I had said during our very first conversation: that one could feel genuine anger only in a situation where one felt certain of acceptance. It had taken him quite some time to recognize and accept how much stubbornness and autonomy I required while we were working our way through the conflicts. Then it had been possible for him, in almost every case, to allow me to take the lead. I had, he told me, rapped his knuckles quite vehemently whenever he tried to grab the reins or to pull them in. He had finally decided to base the working out of conflicts entirely on the principle of voluntarity. Furthermore, and for the first time, he had made it a rule for himself to give in to his own fantasies during longer periods of silence and to regard their content as characteristic of what was going on between us. Indeed, he often surprised me after such a silence, or even at some point when I had been talking again for a while, with the remark: "Let me tell you what *I* have been thinking about while we were quiet." Not only did the most astounding parallels become apparent, but he arrived, by means of what I would like to call a subterranean linkup with my interior events, at highly accurate interpretations. At first, this did not occur without hurt feelings on my part. I often felt that he had not been paying attention, or that he was unloading *his* emotional debris on me instead of listening to me with concentration. When the subterranean channel was not open, and this would happen, either he or I noticed it. Then I would complain: "Once again, you're miles away from me," or he would use the "Uh-huh" as bait to entice me out again, or he asked: "Enjoying the silence?", or said: "Something is preventing you from communicating."

He also told me that he had experimented, and with encouraging results, with the technique of sometimes simply interrupting my trains of thought by communications on observations made in the non-verbal realm, of, e.g., my tone of voice, my facial expression when entering, my posture on the couch, certain gestures. Or he suddenly went back and picked up very early remarks that I had regarded as quasi-accidental, in order to establish a surprising connection. That method requires a solid relationship and a certain tolerance for frustration on the patient's part. In the beginning, I often flew into a rage and yelled at him: "You should be listening to what I'm saying, instead of commenting on my voice or on the way I shook hands with you." At first, it feels like being "found out" in regard to things one did not want to communicate, or which one did not realize one was communicating non-verbally. Yet, as time went on, I became fascinated by the wealth of unconscious forms of expression. After all, I had made the most drastic offer myself right at the beginning, with that open fly. All he really had to do was to stretch out his hand to put it right on the *nervus rerum.*

Finally, he told me a little about his family, his interest in music, his own relationship to father and mother, and some strange parallels became apparent. Quite gradually, he took the shape of a concrete human being whose qualities that I had been intuiting acquired a more real coloration.

The question of our future relations was not easily answered. Although I did not want to admit this to myself, my fantasies had busied themselves during the last months to a great extent with the invention and constellation of possibilities for encounter. This extended from the almost innocent question about supervisors sessions to certain quite sophisticated proposals for collaboration. I had trapped him in all kinds of wishful schemes, cleverly disguised by means of lucid and matter-of-fact arguments. It became evident that I had, with clairvoyant attention, observed the relationships between other analysts and their alumni; that I indulged in fantasies about taking walks and making music together. He obviously did not reject them because of some rigid psychoanalytical morality, but he was concerned to make sure that an undissolved transference would not simply change into a real relationship. In addition, he insisted with conviction that a psychoanalysis of such duration did create a relationship that was subject to similar inherent laws as that between parents and children, where there also are taboo areas of respect and distance, definitely mutual, that have to be taken into account. Thus, the future remains open. But why should I deny that even this book is an attempt to ensnare him a little, to entice him into the durable bonds of friendship?

End of the report

Afterword

1976: An Interim Report

The slow collapse of the illusion that I had emerged from this analysis as an essentially *healed* person was exceedingly painful, embarrassing and humiliating. It confirmed the predictions made by certain colleagues regarding the defensive nature of my idealization of both analyst and analysis. I gained a better understanding of Heinz Kohut's wordplay in his introduction to this book, about the message of salvation changing into one of healing. Unconsciously, I had clung to the psychic model of devoutness and managed to substitute the concept of psycho-analysis for the one of religious truth. The report on a helpful but not really completed analysis had become bastardized with a kind of romanticizing missionary tract, not dissimilar to those some of my ancestors may have distributed to the "heathen" of India or Africa in their time.

About a year after the supposed end of my analysis, I experienced my first severe relapse into a depression that lasted for weeks. I then asked my analyst if he would be willing to resume work with me once again. After a transitional period of several months during which he could give me only one hour a week, the analysis was continued, following a hiatus of almost two years. I think I can best describe the cause of that partial collapse by using the image of that house that he had been helping me to build and to furnish. At question was not a new building but the rehabilitation of an old, *cracked* edifice resting on ancient and largely unknown foundations. During the analysis I had not mustered the courage really to investigate some of the vaulted cellars of the old building. There were certain dungeons whose covered-up entrances I had not even discovered. Others I had seen but had recoiled from, or had covered them up with the many-colored boards of idealization or belief in miracles. Without being aware of it, I let myself be guided by the fear that I might destroy my relationship with the analyst if I allowed the full extent of hatred, mistrust and disdain, as well as the full force of my wishes for symbolic closeness and merging, to gush forth from these dungeons and into the transference. Thus, for years, I repeated a basic childhood pattern with him. In order to be loved, or at least not rejected, one had to suppress certain aspects of one's own person *for ever*. In my fear of rejection, I even managed to deceive the analyst, to guide him right past some of those abysses.

How angry I was with him, then, as we resumed our work, seeing that I had acted towards him for years the way I had acted towards Jocasta and God the Father: splitting myself into a part that was bearable for others and into another one that was so unbearable I had to conceal it absolutely from others, even from myself! This hatred of disappointment raged for several months, as did the anger of shame: to have sung such loud praises of something that now seemed to have been in vain.

The renewed encounter with the buried god image of my childhood, which I had managed to avoid during the analysis and which then inundated me only a few weeks before the resumption of analysis like a subterranean flood, I have described in the small volume titled "God Poisoning". Yet that was only the beginning of a long and difficult journey to find this terrible God again in transference, and to find his associate, the rejecting and condemning mother who constantly overshadowed the kind one; and the sick father, unable to provide sufficient shelter from the combined onslaught by those two.

Since then, there have been many sessions which I truly believed would be the last as the feeling of rejection, unworthiness and hatred seemed to consume all confidence in the durability of our analytical working relationship. Certain very early divisions from the mother have permanently damaged part of the basic capacity for trust. The analysis is still not finished. However, *Apprenticeship* is going into paperback and is appearing in translations, and it would be wrong to let these editions come out without an afterword. In the meantime, it has become clearer to me why *Apprenticeship* is only a little more than half the "truth of the matter."

OTHER BOOKS OF INTEREST PUBLISHED BY URIZEN

LITERATURE

Ehrenburg, Ilya
The Life of the Automobile, novel,
   192 pages
Cloth $8.95 / paper $4.95

Enzensberger, Hans Magnus
Mausoleum, poetry, 132 pages
Cloth $10.00 / paper $4.95

Hamburger, Michael
German Poetry 1910-1975, 576 pages
Cloth $17.50 / paper $6.95

Handke, Peter
Nonsense & Happiness, poetry,
   80 pages
Cloth $7.95 / paper $3.95

Hansen, Olaf (Ed.)
*The Radical Will, Randolph Bourne
(Selected Writings) 1911-1918*
   500 pages
Cloth $17.50 / paper $7.95

Innerhofer, Franz
Beautiful Days, novel, 228 pages
Cloth $8.95 / paper $4.95

Kroetz, Franz Xaver
Farmyard & Other Plays, 192 pages
Cloth $12.95 / paper $4.95

Montale, Eugenio
Poet in Our Time (essays), 96 pages
Cloth $5.95 / paper $2.95

Shepard, Sam
*Angel City, Curse of the Starving
   Class, & Other Plays,* 300 pages
Cloth $15.00 / paper $4.95

FILM

Bresson, Robert
Notes on Cinematography, 132 pages
Cloth $6.95 / paper $2.95

Bresson, Robert
The Complete Screenplays, Vol. I,
   400 pages
Cloth $17.50 / paper $6.95

PSYCHOLOGY

Borneman, Ernest (Ed.)
The Psychoanalysis of Money, 420 pages
Cloth $15.00 / paper $5.95

Doerner, Klaus
Madmen and the Bourgeoisie, 384 pages
Cloth $15.00 / paper $5.95

Patrick C. Lee and Robert S. Stewart
Sex Differences, 500 pages
Cloth $17.50 / paper $5.95

Moser, Tilman
Years of Apprenticeship on the Couch,
240 pages / Cloth $10.00

ECONOMICS

De Brunhoff, Suzanne
Marx on Money, 192 pages
Cloth $10.00 / paper $4.95

Linder, Marc
Anti-Samuelson Vol. I, 400 pages
Cloth $15.00 / paper $5.95
Anti-Samuelson, Vol. II, 440 pages
Cloth $15.00 / paper $5.95

SOCIOLOGY

Andrew Arato/Eike Gebhardt (Eds.)
The Essential Frankfurt School Reader,
544 pages / Cloth $17.50 / paper $5.95

Pearce, Frank
Crimes of the Powerful, 176 pages
Paper $4.95

Van Onselen, Charles
Chibaro (African Mine Labor in Southern
Rhodesia), 368 pages / Cloth $17.50

Shaw, Martin
*Marxism Versus Sociology
   (A Reading Guide),* 120 pages
Cloth $6.95 / paper $2.25

Shaw, Martin
Marxism and Social Science, 125 pages
Paper $2.95

Thönnessen, Werner
The Emancipation of Women, 185 pages
Cloth $10.00 / paper $4.95

Write for a complete catalog to:
Urizen Books, Inc., 66 West Broadway, New York, N.Y. 10007

MAY 1 9 1983